TEXTS UNDER
NEGOTIATION

TEXTS UNDER

NEGOTIATION

The Bible and Postmodern Imagination

Walter Brueggemann

Fortress Press   **Minneapolis**

TEXTS UNDER NEGOTIATION
The Bible and Postmodern Imagination

Interior design: ediType
Cover design: Lecy Design
Cover art: "Planet M" by Mark Saxton

Library of Congress Cataloging-in-Publication Data

Brueggemann, Walter
    Texts under negotiation : the Bible and postmodern imagination /
Walter Brueggemann.
        p. cm.
    Includes bibliographical references and indexes.
    ISBN 0-8006-2736-9 (alk. paper)
    1. Bible—Criticism, interpretation, etc.—History—20th Cent.
I. Title
BS500.B78 1993
220.6'01—dc20   93-18154
                                                                 CIP

The paper used in this publication meets the minimum requirements of American National Standard for Information Sciences—Permanence of Paper for Printed Library Materials, ANSI Z329.48-1984. ∞™

Manufactured in the U.S.A.   AF 1–2736

97   96   95   94   93   1   2   3   4   5   6   7   8   9   10

✦ Contents

✦ | # Preface

THIS BOOK HAS an eminently practical concern, the liberation of the biblical text for the church in a new situation, for interpretation, proclamation, teaching, and practice. There can be little doubt that we are in a wholly new interpretive situation. While this new pluralistic, postmodern situation is perceived by many as a threat to "mainline" churches and to the long-settled claims of conventional text-reading, it is my judgment and my urging that the new situation is in fact a positive opportunity to which church interpreters of the Bible may attend with considerable eagerness.

It is my judgment that church interpretation (especially where historical criticism has been taken with excessive seriousness) has tended to trim and domesticate the text not only to accommodate regnant modes of knowledge, but also to enhance regnant modes of power. (It is here assumed that regnant modes of power and knowledge are always and inextricably intertwined and mutually reinforcing. So Marx: "The ruling ideas of each age have ever been the ideas of its ruling class.")

I have taken some trouble to delineate a postmodern context for interpretation. I have no zeal about the words "modern" and "postmodern" and take them only as a convenient reference for the widespread erosion of what has been most recently seen as "given." While I am unable to define what is "modern," like pornography, I think I know it when I see it. In the practice of biblical interpretation, I have come to think that historical criticism, as conventionally understood, is our particular practice of modernity. This is evident, in my judgment, in the fact that those interpreters who most fear the authoritarianism of the church are most passionate about the positive use of historical criticism, for such criticism was devised precisely as a response against such church authoritarianism.

I have no need or desire to dismiss or overcome historical criticism, for I regard it as a useful (and indispensable) tool. I also believe, however, that a defense against church authoritarianism is not now a clear and present necessity for the larger population of Western society (excepting some important enclaves of eighteenth-century faith that deserve eighteenth-century criticism), and that the main threat to Western society is the tyranny of a positivism that takes political-economic form and that easily co-opts historical criticism. It is interesting to me that those historical critics who most fear the authoritarianism of the church continue to operate out of and react against their own eighteenth-century experience of the church, which is scarcely reflective of what is happening in the church. It may well be that such a stance is of little interest to me because my own nurture and life in the church have seldom been heavy-handed in any ill use of authority. (I am not unaware of the heavy-handed authority of the church that has discriminated against those outside the white, male hegemony; my argument intends to address precisely that undesirable fact.) Thus my statement is not an assault against historical criticism or its world of epistemological power, but only a probe to see how the church in a postcritical context can respond out of the text to a genuine crisis of humanness now besetting belated democratic capitalism. The threat of church authoritarianism has given way to this new crisis. The shoe is now on the other foot. We must learn to "hop" differently.

The three chapters of this book seek to move from the more general to the most specific. The first chapter reflects on the *context* for interpretation, seeking to delineate the political and intellectual winds now blowing. I have no expertise about the historical and philosophical issues involved in the critique of modernity and must take the word of others for some of the argument. Nor do I regard postmodernity as something to welcome, but simply something to acknowledge as the inescapable context in which we live and interpret. I hope I have understood and presented enough to suggest the demands and permissions for interpretation given in and through this context. I will not quibble over labels, but I am convinced that disregard of the new knowledge-power situation in which we find ourselves and of the continued claims of imperial and impervious theological absolutes of a scholastic kind simply will not do, whether the claims are voiced in precritical or critical fashion.

In the second chapter, I have sought to present a provisional *thematization* of the Bible. This is not a particularly new suggestion, except that I have sought to correlate it with the pathological thematization of human experience that is dominant in our consumer economy. In the third chapter, I have moved to quite *specific texts* that assume the foregoing thematization, but that also break beyond it or any thematization. In my judgment, interpretation that can authorize and evoke transformation must always be quite text-specific, even if a thematization hovers in the background. Such specificity is required because that from which transformation is sought is also, in my judgment, characteristically rooted in quite specific "text-scripts." Thematization in and of itself (mine or any other) violates the specificity of the text, even as it is, in my judgment, increasingly incongruous with our emerging knowledge-power situation. Thus the sequence *context—theme—text* is how my mind has worked on these issues. It should be clear to anyone who has thought about these difficult matters that this is a quite provisional presentation. Indeed, I suggest that in any careful assessment of our situation, any offer, made wittingly or not, is surely provisional.

The particular intention of my thinking is that it is the concreteness of the text that holds transformative power. In the large hermeneutical issues before us, this makes clear that my tilt is wholly toward the "Yale School" of Hans Frei and George Lindbeck. I have, however, no great interest in such large wars; nor do I think that the "Yale argument" is sufficiently text-specific. My thinking arises from the bottom up, from congregations (and their ministers) who seek faithful modes of practice.

These lectures were prepared primarily for the Trinity Institute, though I have used some preliminary form of them in other places. The Trinity Institute lectures were delivered in January 1992. All through their preparation and presentation, I was generously supported by Frederic Burnham, director of the institute. During the lectures, I was graciously hosted by Regan Burnham. Time for preparation of the lectures was made possible by a sabbatical leave given by my school, Columbia Theological Seminary, supported by a study grant from the Association of Theological Schools. I am grateful both to Columbia and to the association. My colleague Brian Childs has read the manuscript and made important bibliographic suggestions. As always, it is a delight to work with Marshall Johnson of Fortress Press, who is unfailingly a supportive and helpful editor. Finally, once again, my primal thanks are to Tempie Alexander, who has patiently done the manuscript over and over and over (until she might have written it), with grace and patience commensurate with her great talent.

Chapter	Funding
1	Postmodern
	Interpretation

I
T IS NOW CLEAR TO MANY OF US, in the academy and in the
church, that we are in a quite new interpretive situation
that constitutes something of an emergency. That emergency in interpretation is the result of a radical shift of
categories of culture, for which interpreters of faith in the West
have not been well prepared. It is inevitable that our categories
of interpretation are deeply influenced by and in large part informed by the modes of culture in which they are practiced, as in
every generation. This inescapable reality now concerns us in two
ways.

On the one hand, it was exactly the rise of science and the
resultant epistemology of the Enlightenment that produced interpretation informed by historical criticism.[1] Interpretation informed by historical awareness was such a close and appropriate
match for our context of modernity for the past two hundred
years that we have scarcely been able to notice that the connection is culture-bound and did not always exist. That is, scientific
positivism did not always determine the shape of knowledge, and
historical criticism is not the way in which theological interpretation of Scripture has always proceeded or must proceed.[2] That
close alliance between *modern* context and *"objective"* method,
however, has been decisive in the recent past, both for those who
willingly participated in the critical enterprise and for those who
resisted or followed reluctantly.[3]

On the other hand, there are abundant signs that the dominance of a general scientific positivism is breaking down, and with that breakdown, our modes of theological interpretation from the recent past are less and less pertinent. Thus many commentators say that we are witnessing the "end of modernity," that is, the end of scientific positivism, and with it the end of Enlightenment modes of certitude and certain patterns of political domination. It is disputed whether this ending in fact brings us to "postmodernism" or whether what we now face is simply a move inside modernity, as Jürgen Habermas has proposed. That question, however, need not detain us, for either way, we are in a new interpretive situation that requires of us a new practice of knowledge and a new, derivative option in political power.

In this first chapter, I shall be concerned with more theoretical matters in which I have no particular expertise. I shall proceed by reviewing some recent works that I have found to be informative and suggestive for my own thinking. This theoretical and bibliographical material may seem remote from the practice of ministry and the work of proclamation and liturgy. I shall hope to show, however, that this shift in context decisively changes the shape of the work of ministry. It changes both what is required in ministry and, happily, what is permitted. For that reason I will review in broad sweep the intellectual, cultural developments that bring us to our present situation of interpretation. In my subsequent discussion I shall become more specific and practical, but that more practical consideration depends upon the matters of this first chapter.

• I •

At the beginning of the seventeenth century, in the wake of the Reformation, the intellectual-cultural underpinnings of Western Europe decisively shifted.[4] Those changes, which are regularly associated with the names Descartes, Hobbes, Locke, and Rousseau, among others, saw the collapse of the medieval synthesis in which a coherent, unified system of meaning and power was everywhere pervasive. Note well that I am here deliberately using in the same phrase "meaning" and "power." By "meaning," I refer to a trusted

set of symbols that in that period was constituted by Christian theology. By "power" I mean the capacity to exercise economic and
political control in legitimated ways. By linking the two, I refer
to the long-standing alliance between magisterial symbolization
and political hegemony, namely, the neat fit of *certitude* and *domination.* As the certitude given by the church synthesis began to
weaken, that is, as the claims of the centrist synthesis seemed no
longer beyond reach and no longer absolute, so the capacity to
control also began to weaken. With the loss of certitude and the
loss of domination, life was indeed at risk.

Two books have been particularly informative for my understanding of his drastic and displacing change. Stephen Toulmin,
in *Cosmopolis,* has proposed an extraordinary convergence of fac-
tors around the project of Descartes.[5] Toulmin reports that in the
midst of the terrible European wars of the seventeenth century,
Henry IV of Navarre was the coming king of France. He was a figure
nearly larger than life, who held promise of ending the religious
wars and bringing an ecumenical peace to France and consequently to Europe. Enormously high expectations were attached
to his coming rule. At the brink of his great promise, however, he
was assassinated. Upon his death, so says Toulmin, his heart was
taken as a religious relic and paraded all about France. In the end,
after great public grieving, that relic was brought to La Flèche near
Paris and enshrined with due religious ceremony.

Toulmin observes that the young René Descartes was a student
at that very time in the school where the relic was finally placed.[6]
Toulmin suggests that as the relic of Henry signified the dashing
of enormous hope for a new European peace, so Descartes, along
with his whole generation, was plunged into disarray as the threat
of chaos became a social reality. That is, Descartes's philosophical
reflection was an urgent effort to fend off the coming chaos so
evident in the world around him.[7]

Toulmin's reading of this moment of cultural emergency is sec-
onded by a feminist critique of Descartes by Susan Bordo, in *The
Flight to Objectivity.*[8] In a close reading of Descartes, Bordo has
proposed that Descartes and his cultural world were beset by enormous and profound anxiety as the medieval world collapsed. The
loss of that "home" created deep dislocation and displacement. In
order to respond to that anxiety, Descartes engaged in an intellec-

tual process of individuation, which amounted to separation from "mother" and "loss of mother."

As an alternative to and compensation for the loss of mother ("mother church"? "mother earth"?), Descartes fashioned a new, separated individual consciousness that in fact had no reference point outside itself. This new "interiority" permitted the self to generate its own certitude, and the self became an absolute point of reference.[9] The outcomes of the work of Descartes include:

- "A new model of knowledge grounded in objectivity, and capable of providing a new epistemological security to replace that which was lost in the dissolution of the Medieval world-view."[10]

- The pursuit of "pure reason," free of every contingency, revolved around "the imagery of purity," which meant escaping from all forms of body and earth into the purity of the mind.[11]

- The body and earth as the producers of life thus were seen as peculiarly feminine and material. So Bordo can speak of the "Cartesian masculinization of thought and the flight from the feminine."[12]

It is perhaps not too much in summarizing Bordo to say that a sense of the loss of cosmic mother led Descartes to fashion an impenetrable masculinity that nicely linked "objectivity" and masculine power.

My reason for pausing over Toulmin and Bordo is that they help us understand the new cultural world that was formed in this period, a world that is still with us, but very much in retreat, if not defeat. That world saw the "rise of science," which from the beginning, that is, from Francis Bacon, has been an explicitly masculine enterprise of controlling (and raping) "mother earth."[13] That world also witnessed the remarkable European Reconnaissance, the exploration of the earth and the development of an intricate system of European colonialism that still vexes the world community.[14] The "project of objectivity" nullified tradition (as part of that "failed mothering") and directly aimed at the control of the world.[15]

Thus the new intellectual hegemony of male certitude (unencumbered by the body) fostered a political-economic hegemony, whereby the "disinterested," "objective" ones at the center could dominate the margin. That "objective" control was supremely masculine in its perception and domination.

This enterprise yielded two kinds of reliable knowledge that reinforced each other. On the one hand, knowledge consists in rational, logical coherence, discerned by a detached, disinterested, disembodied mind.[16] On the other hand, knowledge comes from what is experiential, empirical, and factual. In a world where everything is collapsing, something reliable could indeed be established, on the basis of experience. Both Toulmin and Bordo make the case that the Cartesian development (reinforced by Hobbes's absolutism and Locke's empiricism) was not a buoyant act of imagination, but was instead a desperate maneuver to cope with anxiety. Thus "objectivity" emerged as a way to fend off ominous chaos.

Toulmin proceeds to identify the kinds of knowledge that qualify as real knowledge in the horizon of this moment called modernity. He says there was

- a move from oral to *written*, so that what is reliable is what is written;

- a move from the particular to the *universal*, so that real truth is what is true everywhere;

- a move from local to *general*, so that real truth had to be the same from locale to locale; and

- a move from the timely to the *timeless*, so that the real is the unchanging.[17]

Real knowledge is written, universal, general, and timeless; in other words, great truths operate everywhere and thus form a large, coherent whole. In that world, practiced with shameless confidence, there is no need for insecurity, self-doubt, or embarrassment. From the threat of insecurity, this movement arrived at a new, alternative security about itself.

In concluding this foray, I need only observe that theological interpretation has followed nicely along in its modes of certitude. On the one hand, in its rational, logical way, theological method has created a tight system of certitude that purports to be absolute. On the other hand, with its practice of historical criticism, it has sought validation in facticity behind the text. The outcome of such a procedure is that the texts themselves are largely dismissed, and words themselves do not count for much. So there is in modernity a resulting dismissal of rhetoric as "mere rhetoric" and the discounting of speech.[18] I submit that this project that began in anxiety in the seventeenth century is still very much with us. It has very much determined the church's modes of certitude and its collusion in domination in this most masculine world offered by science.

• II •

A number of critics now suggest that the modes of certitude and domination that arose in the seventeenth and eighteenth centuries were not an irreversible change, but in fact were an episode or "project," that is, a deliberate human achievement that could be sustained for a very long time, but not an ultimate transformation. Thus it is now argued that the modes of certitude and domination reflected by the Enlightenment and sustained for a very long time are a spent force that no longer commands authority or allegiance. (Such a statement is clearly an overstatement, because these modes of perception, articulation, and practice are very deep among us and are not easily abandoned or readily transformed.)

Toulmin's own analysis ends with a compelling argument that we can now see the reversal of the process of modernity, as we move from

> written to oral,
> universal to particular,
> general to local, and
> timeless to timely.[19]

Toulmin proposes that we increasingly accept as true and valid what is oral, particular, local, and timely.

In a very different way, Langdon Gilkey identifies four facets of the profound change we face:[20]

1. *Intellectual* know-how (and its resultant technology) has failed to deliver the good life and has "revealed itself not only as ambiguous but also as potentially lethal in its consequences."[21]

What seemed good has turned out to be enormously ambiguous in its fruit.

2. The *political* promise of the Enlightenment has failed to bring peace and has led to powerful tyranny sustained by ideology.

3. "Salvation history has collapsed." Gilkey observes that with Western culture as the carrier of good in its struggle with evil, "a good case can be made that the spiritual substance of the Enlightenment took its shape *against* the Hebrew and the Christian myths or salvation history."[22] Said another way, the claim of "progress" has not worked out at all convincingly.

4. Confrontation with world religions has shaken the monopolistic claim of Western religions that are closely allied with the Enlightenment and with its forms of domination.

These four features together place us, as heirs of this project, in a peculiar jeopardy, about which I will comment later.[23]

Before moving on, however, I want to cite four other studies that have addressed the crisis of objective certitude.

The most important of these is *The Structure of Scientific Revolutions,* by Thomas Kuhn.[24] In an influential—I believe classic—study, Kuhn has argued that science does not proceed simply by the careful accumulation of data that lead to new insight. Rather, scientific data are organized around models or paradigms that have a capacity to gather to themselves and accommodate an enormous amount of data. Change in our discernment happens when through a daring political act, a new paradigm is articulated, it receives influential support in the scientific community, the data are dramatically transported by its practitioners from one paradigm to another, and a new "scheme" (theory) of knowledge becomes authoritative. That is, scientific knowledge is to some extent a political achievement whereby power is utilized to shape perception and interpretation in one direction rather than in another.[25] To the extent that scientific knowledge is a political, rhetorical achievement, it is not objective in any positivistic sense. That is, the interest of the knower intrudes powerfully into what is known.

In an older, gentler, but revolutionary book, *Personal Knowledge,* Michael Polanyi has argued that knowledge, even scientific knowledge, has a decisive fiduciary element.[26] That is, knowing requires great trust in the knowing already done by others, which means that knowledge is to some extent an enterprise of human construction, and not simply a matter of flat objectivity.

Richard Rorty, an extreme advocate of deconstruction, has observed that objectivity is an agreement of everyone in the room.[27] The problem is that in the great career of Western objectivity very few people were let into the room, which was peopled largely by white males of a certain class and perspective.[28] Indeed, it has been precisely the admission of others into the room that has made our treasured objectivity (and consequent hegemony) fragile and exposed.

Jean-François Lyotard, in *The Post-modern Condition*, has made the extreme case that no "grand story" can any longer claim assent; he asserts that we are left only with quite local stories, thus picking up an accent of Toulmin.[29]

One does not need to embrace all of these analyses in order to sense that we face a decisive turn in our ways of knowing. Even if the case for postmodernity is considerably overstated, it is nonetheless important that this kind of conversation is now thought to be possible or necessary. It is likely that of the scholars I have mentioned, especially Rorty and Lyotard go much farther than many of us would go. My point is not to persuade for or advocate their program. My more modest intent is to insist that we are in a new interpretive situation that requires and permits the interpreters of the church to work at a different task.

It is clear on many fronts, not only in theology but in very many disciplines, that the old modes of knowing that are Euro-American, male, and white, no longer command respect and credibility as objective and universally true. Indeed, older modes of assertion about reality have an increasingly empty ring, even if we do not understand all the reasons for the change.

In place of objective certitude and settled hegemony, we would now characterize our knowing in ways that make mastery and control much more problematic, if indeed mastery and control can any longer be our intention at all. I would characterize our new intellectual situation in these rather obvious ways:

1. Our knowing is inherently *contextual*. This should hardly come to us as a surprise. Descartes wanted to insist that context was not relevant to knowing. It is, however, now clear that what one knows and sees depends upon where one stands or sits.

This matter of contextualism is of particular interest to those who practice something like a "liberation hermeneutic."[30] Indeed, such voices are often dismissed as "context-conditioned." Such voices of interpretation, however, do not pretend otherwise; they do not deny the power of context in their discernment. They want to insist only that as their own view is contextual, so also is every other view, including those that claim to be objective and noncontextual. Contextualism argues that the knower helps constitute what is known, that the socioeconomic-political reality of the knower is decisive for knowledge.

2. It follows that contexts are quite *local*, and the more one generalizes, the more one loses or fails to notice context.[31] Localism means that it is impossible to voice large truth. All one can do is to voice local truth and propose that it pertains elsewhere. In fact, I should insist that all our knowing is quite local, even when we say it in a loud voice. So that even the teaching of "the universal church," whether Rome or Canterbury or Geneva, is quite local. Conversely, knowledge is notoriously parochial, even if it is the provincialism of those who stand at the center and dominate.

3. It follows from contextualism and localism that knowledge is inherently *pluralistic*, a cacophony of claims, each of which rings true to its own advocates.[32] Indeed, pluralism is the only alternative to objectivism once the dominant center is no longer able to impose its view and to silence by force all alternative or dissenting opinion.[33]

Thus I shall want to argue that the practice of Christian interpretation in preaching and liturgy is *contextual, local,* and *pluralistic.* We voice a claim that rings true in our context, that applies authoritatively to our lived life. But it is a claim that is made in a pluralism where it has no formal privilege.

We are now able to see that what has passed for objective, universal knowledge has in fact been the interested claim of the dominant voices who were able to pose their view and to gain either assent or docile acceptance from those whose interest the claim did not serve.[34] Objectivity is in fact one more practice of ideology that presents interest in covert form as an established fact.[35]

I am aware that this argument of contextualism, localism, and pluralism will strike some as a statement of relativism, as though any one claim is as good as any other. To this, I make two responses. First, I am not *advocating* an end to objectivity, but only describing how it is with us. The truth is that there is no answer in the back of the book to which there is assent, no final arbiter who will finally adjudicate rival claims. Moreover, those who want absolutes tend to accept authority only if it speaks the absolute claim to which they are already disposed before anything has been said. In fact, we are in a situation in which all the rival claims are present to us at the same time, without any transcendent arbiter. Even if we wish it were different, it is not.

Second, the threat of unbridled relativism is not, in my judgment, much of a threat. In reality, the dispute boils down to a few competing claims on any issue, and this is not the same as "anything goes." I regard relativism as less of a threat than objectivism, which I believe to be a very large threat among us precisely because it is such a deception. I find it helpful, over against the real threat of objectivism and the lesser danger of relativism, to attend to the practice of *perspectivism,* which I believe is what Kuhn and Polanyi have intended.[36] That is, the world is perceived, processed, and articulated with one or another perspective, and a perspective has the power to make sense out of the rawness of experienced life, even though it cannot be "proven" or absolutely established.

In Christian faith, the specific form faith takes is of a certain ilk, practiced from a certain perspective that one embraces in the face of other, rival perspectives. Such advocacy in conversation seeks to listen carefully to other perspectives.[37] It holds before the conversation a certain posture on reality. This posture does not claim to be objectively true, but it claims to be a position where one will stand at cost and at risk, so that in the end, the test of its validity is no longer logic or fact, but the expenditure of one's own life, which is the only thing that finally has worth.[38] Thus I propose that the shift from an *objective claim of hegemony* to a *contextual, local perspective* accurately describes our pastoral situation. We may not like it, and folk may not acknowledge it, but it is so.

Before moving on to a more constructive comment, let me indicate three aspects of this change from hegemony to perspective that I believe touch directly upon pastoral reality.

1. The large, experienced reality faced daily by those with

whom we minister is the collapse of the white, male, Western world of colonialism. While that world will continue to make its claim for a very long time, its unchallenged authority and credibility are over and done with. This new reality touches each of us in threatening and frightening ways. It touches the economy and reaches right into our patterns of employment and retirement.[39] It touches home and domestic authority in families. And as our systems of management and control break down, the collapse makes us at least anxious and perhaps greedy, and in the end it leads to a justification of many kinds of brutality. The experience of this collapse is profound, intense, and quite concrete. There is a lot of political mileage in rhetoric that pretends the old system works, but it is a deception.[40] Thus the end of modernity, I propose, is not some remote, intellectual fantasy, but reaches down into the lives of folk like us.

2. While the visible effect of the failure of modernity is practical, that is to say, economic and political, it touches no less our theology. As we experience the loss of the universal, something happens to our capacity to make large, grand claims for God's sovereignty, which have been characteristically expressed in virile terms.[41] I am aware that the Reformed tradition has staked a good deal on a high view of God's "sovereignty." I am aware also that even that claim in the sixteenth century was contextual in the face of the collapse of the medieval synthesis. That is, Calvin made that claim against the failing moral sovereignty and legitimacy of the Roman church.[42] The recent articulation of God's pathos reflects an uneasiness about such a macho God at the edge of modernity.[43] Moreover, the argument about inclusive language for God reflects the collapse, or at least disease, of a Cartesian masculinization of faith. Thus our articulation of God will need to begin again in local, contextual ways—ways, I suggest, that are peculiarly congenial to Jewish modes of speech.[44]

3. Less important but worth noting, the end of modernity requires a critique of method in scripture study. It is clear to me that conventional historical criticism is, in scripture study, our particular practice of modernity, whereby the text was made to fit our modes of knowledge and control.[45] As we stand before the text, no longer as its master but as its advocate, we will have to find new methods of reading.

I suggest that on all three counts:

- the pastoral crisis of social displacement,
- the theological crisis of respeaking God, and
- the methodological crisis of how to read,

pastors of the church have before them a major piece of work. In what follows, I will also want to insist that the church and its pastors need no longer submit to the dominant modes of power and certitude, and so stand in a place of great freedom, freedom to be our confessing selves in a faithful community, as modernity has not permitted us to be (see Gal. 5:1).

• III •

This shift *from hegemony to perspective,* I shall argue, is an enormous opportunity for Christian ministry. The shift entails a recovery of recognition *speech* as decisive for our existence. Hegemony, intellectual and political, as it always does, had eliminated probing speech, daring rhetoric, and subversive text, and had insisted that reality is a settled matter that language can describe, but upon which it cannot actively impinge.[46] Our new intellectual environment acknowledges that human agents are in process of constituting reality, and that formative work is done through rhetoric.[47] This means that speech is not merely descriptive, but it is in some sense evocative of reality and constitutive of reality. Indeed, even the older assertion that speech only describes is itself an act of advocacy. That claim did not appear to be an act of advocacy because all counteradvocacies were driven from the field by the domination textured as objectivity.

But consider how our circumstance and our responsibility are changed if our embrace of reality consists in the persuasive advocacy and adjudication of competing construals, perspectives, and paradigms of reality! Speech becomes decisive for reality, for speech pictures, portrays, imagines, and authorizes reality in this way and not in some other.

The great shift in interpretive practice I want to consider is that in this post-Cartesian situation, knowing consists not in settled

certitudes but in the actual work of imagination.[48] By imagination, I mean very simply the human capacity to picture, portray,
receive, and practice the world in ways other than it appears to
be at first glance when seen through a dominant, habitual, unexamined lens. More succinctly, imagination as the quintessential
human act is a valid way of knowing. Imagination as a human act
does not yield the kind of certitude required by Cartesian anxiety,
but it does yield a possible "home" when we accept a participating role as "home-maker."[49] Notice that this is not an argument
for right brain/left brain matters, which I believe to be yet another version of Cartesian dualism.[50] I submit that the whole of the
human brain-mind-spirit has a capacity for imaginative construal,
and so the issue of imagination cannot be grasped according to
the usual dualisms that are endlessly listed and repeated in "bi-
nomial ideology." Thus all knowing, I insist, including "male,"
right-brain knowing, is imaginative construal, even if disguised
or thought to be something else. The world we take as "given"
is a long-established act of imagination that appeals to be and
claims assent as the only legitimate occupant of the field. It follows, then, that long-imagined "givens" can indeed be challenged,
and a "countergiven" is entertainable. (I take this to be the point of
Kuhn's "new paradigm," and I will argue it is the point of Christian
proclamation that aims at conversion.)[51]

We may pause to notice an explosion of recent literature that is
not militantly or even explicitly postmodern, but which concerns
imagination as a valued and authoritative practice of epistemology.

1. Mary Warnock's *Imagination,*[52] a forerunner of the subsequent explosion of books in this area, is a quite practical book. It
provides a history of imagination as an intellectual option, pausing over Kant and considering especially the work of Samuel Taylor
Coleridge, who stands as a primary reference point on this subject
in the modern world. Warnock's work culminates in an argument
concerning British education, making the case that the state has
a stake in education that aims at the nurture and legitimation of
imagination.[53]

2. *Imagining God,* by Garrett Green, has been for me the most
important of these books, no doubt because I read it at the right
moment.[54] Green traverses the history of imagination in a fashion parallel to that of Warnock. But Green, unlike Warnock, has

a theological interest. I single out two points that seem to me to be critical.

First, Green asserts that the canon of Scripture provides the paradigm through which the faithful practice imagination.[55] This concern for canon reflects his Yale education with Hans Frei and George Lindbeck, perhaps with the influence of Brevard Childs. There are, to be sure, difficulties in an appeal to canon, partly because the notion of canon means something very different to a systematic theologian who tends to regard Scripture in a necessarily reductionist way. It is nonetheless important that Green treats the text as the material substance and arena for the practice of imagination. I shall argue that Christian preaching and proclamation are essentially an enterprise of imagining the world through the rhetoric of this text.

Second, and most important, Green identifies "as" as the "copula of imagination."[56] It is conventional to appeal to Paul's injunction to Christians to live "as if . . ." (1 Cor. 7:29-31). The problem with "as if" is that the phrase clearly acknowledges that the practice of faith is contrary to *fact*. That is, act other than life really is. Such an assertion concedes everything to some other "given," which stands over against and behind the Christian act. By contrast, "as" makes no such concession. Thus the injunction to live "*as* free persons" means to accept one's status as free and to live that way, no matter how much some dominant social definition may cast one as "slave." That is, the "as" of freedom intentionally and frontally contradicts and refuses the "as" of slavery.

This "as"—which concedes nothing to another, rival "as," but embraces a different claim of reality, namely, a different construal of reality—has two functions. On the one hand, it exercises a critical, negative function. It rejects "as false" the "as" that has been long accepted and habituated. On the other hand, positively, it asserts a new "as" and proceeds to act upon it, "as though" it were not "as" but "is." That is, the act of "as" proceeds to a new "is." It accepts an alternative construal of reality as a legitimate and valid one, thereby displacing another "as" that is the imposed work of some other act of imagination.

Let us take a case in point. If we ask what the Gulf War of 1991 was, we may take it

- *as* a maintenance of order by the international community,

- *as* the protection of self-determination for Kuwait,

- *as* the defense of cheap oil,

- *as* George Bush's act of machismo, to shed the "wimp" label,

- *as* a mop-up for the British Empire in the Middle East, or

- *as* the defense of the state of Israel.

Formally, any one of these "ases" has as much credence as any other. None has privilege, and there is no ultimately right definition. Each is an act of interpretive construal that is in part argued and in part simply asserted, but which becomes a basis and warrant for policy decisions. A postmodern climate recognizes that there is no given definition and that the rival claims must simply be argued out.

I am especially interested in the critical, subversive function of this imaginative "as." In the work of Kuhn, Rorty, and Lyotard, it is recognized that the long-established "givens" will prevail because they are accepted as beyond criticism. They will prevail until a counter-"as" is imagined and voiced. It is astonishing how a long-established "as" can keep people in their social place, and how daring an alternative "as" can be in changing social relationships and the power that keeps them unchanged.[57]

I labor this point because I want to insist that the Christian gospel is a counter-"as" to the long-accepted "as" that is widely and uncritically accepted as objectively real. I cite only one example that brings together Green's points on canon as paradigm and on the counter-"as." In Luke 13:10-17, Jesus comes upon a woman who has been crippled for eighteen years: "She was bent over and was quite unable to stand up straight." Jesus invites her to stand up straight, and he lays his hands on her. In verse 16, Jesus calls her a "daughter of Abraham," one in whose body the promises of God are powerfully at work. Her social context had construed her otherwise—crippled, dysfunctional, and worthless. She, moreover, had accepted that debilitating "as" for her life.

Jesus counters that "as" out of the old text of Genesis, renames her, and imagines her otherwise. She accepts his counterverdict:

"She stood up straight and began praising God" (v. 13). Note well that Jesus' power is rooted at least in part in this old Abrahamic text to which he dares appeal in a context where the text had long ago been domesticated and dismissed. Jesus enacts a magisterial "as" that, before the witnesses' very eyes, functions as an "is."[58] He refuses to accept the givens of his context and voices a different reality that is borne on the countertext.[59]

3. David Bryant's *Faith and the Play of Imagination*[60] in important ways parallels the work of Garrett Green. In one important way, however, Bryant's argument seems to me an advance over Green's. Green has proposed that we "see as," which is essentially a passive posture of receiving what is given. Bryant proposes not only that we "see as," but that we "take as," thus suggesting a more active, constructive position. That is, to "take as" means to assert, claim, and redefine. To be sure, there is a danger of excessive constructivism, as though one did not need to honor what is there and what is in fact given. But what is there and given is amazingly supple and subject to reconstrual. The problem is that our unintentional "taking" is so well-established that we fail to notice how constructed it is. (The "place of women" is a case in point. Until someone "took" it differently, women had to "take" their place.) My student Tod Linafelt has nicely suggested that Green and Gordon Kaufman reflect extreme positions on imagination. Whereas Green is largely receptive, Kaufman is exclusively constructivist.[61] Bryant, in a careful, mediating way, does not overstate the constructive possibility, but gives considerable latitude for the "taking" of initiative in redefining reality. It is my judgment that every forceful speech, every act of advocacy, is in a powerful way a constructive "taking as." In what follows, I shall suggest that Christian proclamation is an offer that the world may be "taken" differently.

4. Richard Kearney, in *The Wake of Imagination*, has traversed the same ground of the history of imagination considered by Warnock and Green.[62] Kearney's particular interest, however, is in ethics. He proposes that ethical thought can no longer be descriptively absolutist or positivistic. Instead, ethical thought must be admittedly an act of imagination. He proposes that imagination must be *critical* and *poetic*, and then *ethical.* That is, the shaping of social reality is largely determined by the modes of discourse

and by the kinds of questions put in the act of imagination. Notice that Kearney does not appeal to criteria outside the process
of imagination, but wants to recharacterize the potential work of
imagination.[63]

5. Finally, in *Teaching and Religious Imagination*,[64] Maria Harris, a foremost Roman Catholic educational theorist, has provided
a quite practical reflection upon the work of imagination in educational nurture and maturation. Under the general rubric of
imagination, she proposes that education must "take risks, take
care, take steps, take time, and take form."

There is obviously a great deal more to be learned from these
several books, and I commend them to my readers. Notice that
with the exception of Warnock, all of these books come from a
brief, recent period, a period that reflects an abrupt awareness of
the new situation in which theological work finds itself. It may
be that "postmodern" is too particular or too ambitious a word
for what is being noticed. That word, however, is useful to point
to the changed epistemological context in which we must now do
our work. Theological thinkers have come to see, on the one hand,
that theology can no longer make absolute claims in a vacuum and
expect ready assent. On the other hand, this shift in categories indicates the reluctance of theology to accept any longer a muted
position of marginality assigned it by the dominant position of
other intellectual claims of both positivistic science and positivistic
politics.

The new mode of theology now permitted and required reflects an acknowledgment that all claims of reality, including those
by theologians, are fully under negotiation. Theological discourse
is prepared to and capable of participation in these negotiations,
no longer pretending to be a privileged insider, no longer willing
to be a trivialized outsider. Reality, so far as our social conversation is concerned, is no longer a fixed arrangement inhospitable
to theological categories, but it is an ongoing, creative, constitutive
task in which imagination of a quite specific kind has a crucial role
to play.[65] The core of our new awareness is that the world we have
taken for granted in economics, politics, and everywhere else is an
imaginative construal. And if it is a construal, then from any other
perspective, the world can yet be construed differently. It is the
claim of our faith, and the warrant for our ministry, to insist that

our peculiar memory in faith provides the materials out of which an alternatively construed world can be properly imagined.[66]

• IV •

I want now to turn this rather abstract reflection much more closely toward the practice of ministry. The *formal premise* I urge is that our knowing is essentially imaginative, that is, an act of organizing social reality around dominant, authoritative images. This means that the assumptions that have long had unexamined privilege among us are now seen to be sturdy, powerful acts of imagination, reinforced, imposed, and legitimated by power.

On the basis of this formal premise, I assert the *substantive claim* that the practice of modernity, of which we are all children, since the seventeenth century has given us a world imagined through the privilege of white, male, Western, colonial hegemony, with all its pluses and minuses. It is a world that we have come to trust and take for granted as a given. It is a world that has wrought great good, but that has also accomplished enormous mischief against some for the sake of others.[67] The simple truth is that this construed world can no longer be sustained, is no longer persuasive or viable, and we are able to discern no large image to put in its place.

Let me remind the reader that I intend this judgment to be descriptive. It is not a recommendation, or a proposal, or a celebration. Moreover, the loss of this long-valued world is not a gain for liberals over against conservatives, nor a gain for conservatives over against liberals. It is simply, I propose, the great social reality of our time and place. We are unable to detect fully why this long-established imaginative construal should now, at this particular juncture, be exhausted. It may be exhausted simply because it has had a long run, a longer run than any to which it was entitled, a run since the time of Descartes, Hobbes, and Locke. It may be that it is God's own spirit that is causing its demise and collapse, for this is indeed a God "who brings to nought the things that exist" (1 Cor. 1:28). It may be that its demise is the result of the rise of revolutionary expectations, of the growing sense of self-consciousness, of the restless insistence upon rights, and of the insistent voice now recovered by non-Christian cultures and non-Christian religions against the hegemony of the Christian West. This growing sense of self-consciousness is indeed a product of the Enlightenment itself, so that the Enlightenment may contain within itself the impetus for the demise of the Euro-American hegemony it served so well. The reasons for the collapse are many and complex.[68]

This much I know: The imagined world of privilege and disparity is treasured by all of us who live in the advantaged West. It is treasured more by men than by women, more by whites than by blacks, but all of us in the West have enormous advantage. The loss of that world, it follows, is enormously frightening and disturbing to us all, if we notice or think about it. Our fear invites us to gestures of nostalgia, and it reduces us to acts of brutality. I submit that this loss is very large in its sociopolitical scope, touching great strategic questions. But it is also as intimate, personal, and interpersonal as one's own household. Specifically, I suggest that the tired arguments in the church concerning homosexuality are largely a respectable point at which to quarrel about the loss of our known world, rather like the mindless debate about who in the State Department "lost China." Thus, I propose that the discussion of homosexuality, for the most part, is not about sexuality, but is about the reordering of social power, the fearful effort to maintain conventional forms of power that carry less and less conviction, and the awareness that the old center "will not hold."

It is my thesis that our context for ministry is the *failure of the imagination of modernity,* in both its moral-theological and its economic-political aspects. We are at a moment when the imagination of modernity is being displaced by postmodern imagination, which is less sure and less ambitious and which more modestly makes a local claim. That postmodern act of imagination must work its way in the presence of other, rival, and competing acts of imagination, none of which can claim any formal advantage or privilege. Thus, at its deepest levels, our culture is one in which the old imagined world is lost, but still powerfully cherished, and in which there is bewilderment and fear, because there is no clear way on how to order our shared imagination differently or better.

Now, my theme is not postmodern imagination. My topic is a more modest one: *funding* postmodern imagination. It is not, in my judgment, the work of the church (or of the preacher) to construct a full alternative world, for that would be to act as preemptively and imperialistically as all those old construals and impositions. Rather, the task is to *fund*—to provide the pieces, materials, and resources out of which a new world can be imagined. Our responsibility, then, is not a grand scheme or a coherent system, but the voicing of a lot of little pieces out of which people can put life together in fresh configurations. These little pieces of evangelical faith, which constitute the material the church voices, have a certain pull or inclination about how they flow together, and some modestly larger constructs seem to be almost unavoidable for this material. Or at least some construals are more faithful to the material than other construals. I shall insist, however, that the work of funding consists not in the offer of a large, ordered coherence, but in making available lots of disordered pieces that admit of more than one large ordering.

I propose, then, a relook, in a postmodern context, at what the meeting of liturgy and proclamation is all about. That meeting is not, in my urging, a place to come to affirm the great absolutes that are allied with a modernist hegemony. It is not a place for claims that are so large and comprehensive that they ring hollow in a context of our general failure, demise, and disease. It is rather a place where people come to receive new materials, or old materials freshly voiced, that will fund, feed, nurture, nourish, legitimate, and authorize a *counterimagination of the world.*

Note well my insistence here that this is an act of *counter*-imagination. It is not imagination that is at all congenial to dominant intellectual or political modes. It does not easily conform to either the revolutionary or the reactionary advocates of our world. When it comes, it makes no accommodation to the epistemological assumptions or social biases of the congregation. It is, however, a nervy offer of a world in and through a radically different perspective. It is my judgment that the low-energy of the church and the fatigue of many clergy come about because we begin by making too many concessions to the dominant epistemology around us. We make these concessions because we know we will not get much of a hearing otherwise, or because we ourselves have this incredulous, sinking feeling about the claims we are about to utter.

But consider what would emerge if the clergy accepted as

their modest role the voicing of scripture material, without ex-cessive accommodating—that is, without accommodation to what is politically acceptable or morally conventional, without accom-modation to political liberalism or political reactionism, without accommodation to religious orthodoxy or critical urbaneness, but only uttered the voice of the text boldly, as it seems to present itself, even though it does not seem to connect to anything.

I will try to clarify how this notion of *funding* might play out if put into practice. The analogue I find helpful is the function of a powerful ego-structure and the act and experience of psycho-therapy. (I do not intend at all to reduce ministry to therapy, but only to suggest that the modes of discourse and interaction in therapy are richly suggestive.) Three things happen in talk-therapy that illumine our concern. First, therapeutic talk, when it is serious, does not concern large, schematic settlements of one's life, but depends upon going underneath the visible structures of self to the little, specific details that hold hidden power over us. Thus one waits to hear again one specific conversation in which one can recall the exact wording that was so crucial. And out of these little bitty pieces of memory may come the stuff of new self-discernment, and eventually, of new self. That recovered con-versation, however, is characteristically heard only a little at a time, without any large sense of where one is going. Over time these little pieces may amount to an enormous challenge to one's ego-structure, and if one is blessed, they contain the hint of a massive reordering of one's self.

Second, the therapist does not have to see everything or know everything in advance. It is enough to surface and hold and honor the little pieces, to savor their potentially revelatory power, to let the true subject of these little pieces make judgments. In parallel fashion, the pastor does not see and know everything in advance, but lives patiently and faithfully while the new pieces of disclosure surface and do their work. Pascal, in the very face of Descartes, observed that an insight for self is superior to one imposed from somewhere else.

Third, one need not too narrowly construe Freud's dictum that dreams are "the royal road" to the unconscious. It is enough, for our purposes, to observe that it is the unguarded rumination, without focus or disciplined meaning, that may trigger an insight, a connection, an illumination that liberates and heals. Such therapeutic conversation is exceedingly difficult for those of us who are too sure, too settled, too established. *Mutatis mutandis*, in the church, we have often a gathering of seemingly settled people. We may be settled into old scholasticisms or old liturgical habits. We may be settled into a thin suburban morality of competence and success. Or we may be powerfully into an orthodoxy of liberal social causes. In any of these options, everything may be settled before we come to the meeting.[69] In the face of that settlement, the minister offers an old, angular text, freighted with contradictory embarrassment. The text does not seem to fit, or to carry meaning. At the first hint of that threat of the text, we respond defensively, "No, that's not important." But then we walk about the text, turn it to listen again, and find ourselves surprisingly addressed and opened. It is not for nothing that scholars have suggested that Freud's work is not unlike older work in Jewish midrash, for the latter dares to imagine a wild textuality that carries and voices more than we can entertain.[70]

So consider the preacher, standing in front of a congregation, frightened to death with the congregation, because the old world is gone forever. The preacher comes to this meeting without great resources, only this odd, hoary text. What happens is that in this meeting:

- old, neglected texts from Genesis and Chronicles and Philippians are read, and at first they seem removed and modest;

- the preacher says more than she or he knows because folk are listening and doing some of the work, rehearing and reorienting both the coming text and their listening lives;

- old settlements and certitudes are undercut, and awesome playfulness is voiced where our own marginality can surface unafraid; and

- the preacher has provided memories and narratives and visions and images and metaphors that are not easily domesticated or co-opted. They linger in the hearing, and in the conversation that does not end with the benediction. They continue, powered by the Spirit, to do some of their own work.

So consider the meeting where the minister presides. Everyone arrives there with a presumed, taken-for-granted world, perhaps not recognized or consciously valued, but operative, a world with assumptions about money and sex, about Communists and daughters-in-law, about a new lawn mower, about Vietnamese boat people, about college basketball and a birthday gift and the famine in Ethiopia. It is a world unexamined, but passionately held.

The action of the meeting begins—music, word, prayer, theater. At its center, the minister reads (or has read) these very old words, remote, archaic, something of a threat, something of yearning. In the listening, one hears another world proposed. It is an odd world of "no male or female," of condemned harlots and welcomed women, of sheep and goats judged, of wheat and tares tolerated, of heavy commandments and free grace, of food given only for work, and widows and orphans valued in their nonproductivity. If one listens long and hard, what emerges is a different world. Of course, I will not listen long and hard, for my mind wanders. I doze and am distracted, but the sounds keep coming.

If the minister does not trim the text down too much, but voices its angular words, clearly some of this ill fits me. The *proposed world* offered in the text runs dead against my *presumed world* that seems to function less and less effectively. On occasion, I am upset, awed, angry, forlorn, attracted. On my plate is more than one world, some presumed, some proposed, and then comes music, liminality, and adjudication. The minister has respected me, like Pascal knew he must, has not come too close, has given me room, but has been unflinching, unaccommodating, uncompromising in showing me texts that do not fit, dreams that expose my skewed ego-structure and invite me to run beyond myself, that is to say, my old self.

This meeting of course is not the whole of my life, or even a large piece of it. The church is not the only body that knows we are postmodern, postsystem, postcertitude. The preacher is not the only one seeking to provide new material for my imagination, for I am addressed by "legion" in diverse and odd ways. In this moment, however, the preacher is granted complete priority and a fully attended hearing. In this moment, I am agreed to give my

attention to this option; the preacher must take care not to com-
promise but to stay very close to the odd text that is the source
of this proposed alternative. As I come to this meeting, I am not
unlike a person who enters a psychotherapeutic conversation. On
the one hand, such a person wants the therapist to know; but on
the other hand, the person cringes, for the therapist may find out.
In this conversation, I desperately want the minister to speak the
text in its full power, but I also want very much to have the text
toned down to make it more palatable. I come to the meeting hop-
ing and fearing, willing to be addressed, to see if there are indeed
new resources and new possibilities.

The purpose of preaching and of worship is transformation.[71]
We undertake theater that is potentially life-changing. This is the
meeting. This is where the transformative action takes place. This
is not talk about some other meeting somewhere else. This dramatic moment intends that folk should go away changed, perhaps
made whole, perhaps savaged. Because the meeting intends transformation, a crucial question for us is, How do people change?
How have we in our own lives been changed? While the process of
change is complex and usually hidden, we note that a postmodern
context operates on the assumption that our life is indeed supple
and more or less open.[72] I would argue:

1. People do not change, or change much, because of doctrinal
argument or sheer cognitive appeal. Perhaps in a different cultural
climate doctrine has wrought change, but I think not among us. I
believe that doctrine is important, but its practical function is to
provide reflective justification for the reality of life that is lived and
trusted at a more experiential, intimate level.

2. People do not change, or change much, because of moral
appeal. Perhaps in a different cultural climate it has happened, but
I think not among us. I believe that moral appeal is important, but
its pastoral function is to provide a coherent and communal point
of reference in the midst of which we process hopes and fears that
are embarrassing and mostly kept hidden.

3. I shall argue that in a conversation wherein doctrinal argument and moral suasion are operative, people in fact change by the
offer of new models, images, and pictures of how the pieces of life
fit together—models, images, and pictures that characteristically
have the particularity of narrative to carry them. Transformation is

the slow, steady process of inviting each other into a counterstory about God, world, neighbor, and self. This slow, steady process has as counterpoint the subversive process of unlearning and disengaging from a story we find no longer to be credible or adequate.

There are, to be sure, large epistemological issues related to the matters I have explicated. There are, no doubt, difficulties in the schematic distinction of modernity and postmodernity. Granted all of that complexity, however, I nonetheless insist that our church situation in preaching and liturgy is a quite new one. One does not need to honor the old absolute system of modernity. This creates an uncommon freedom for the text of Scripture and for our own construal of the world through what we "take" to be the live word of God (on "taking" see above p. 16).

What is yearned for among us is not new doctrine or new morality, but new world, new self, new future. The new world is not given whole, any more than the new self is given abruptly in psychotherapy. It is given only a little at a time, one text at a time, one miracle at a time, one poem, one healing, one pronouncement, one promise, one commandment. Over time, these pieces are stitched together into a sensible collage, stitched together, all of us in concert, but each of us idiosyncratically, stitched together in a new whole—all things new!

The crisis of modernity and postmodernity, the shift from hegemony to perspective, poses questions for the ministry of the church:

Have we ourselves enough nerve, freedom, and energy to move beyond the matrix of modernity and its confident, uncritical wholeness to trust the concreteness of this text?

Have we enough confidence in the biblical text to let it be our fund for counterimagination?

A no to these questions, in my judgment, consigns the church to disappear with the rest of modernity. A yes can be liberating for the church as a transformational body, liberating even for its ministers who must stand up and imagine.

| Chapter 2 | The Counterworld of Evangelical Imagination |

N A POSTMODERN WORLD where neither the old orthodoxies nor the more recent positivisms will hold, the preacher's chance (both task and opportunity) is to construct, with and for the congregation, an evangelical infrastructure that makes a different communal life possible. In this chapter I want to explore the construction of that infrastructure.

· I ·

Four preliminary points are in order:

1. I use the word "evangelical" in its proper sense as an adjectival form of "gospel." I do not mean to allude to any current popular religious notion of "evangelicals" with a long *e*. I refer to a mode of life, faith, and discourse that lives in deep tension with every faith option that does not mediate active rescue from our common deathliness.

2. I assume, and will not argue here, that the stuff of an evangelical infrastructure is the text of the Bible. I take this in a quite specific way, even while I am not unaware of the great ideological problems with the material of the Bible itself. I want to insist that, taken as baldly as possible on its own terms, the Bible does indeed radically reconstrue and recontextualize reality. Moreover, this reconstrual and recontextualization are profoundly evangeli-

cal, even in those parts of the text that are on first reading visible antigospel.

3. I use the term "infrastructure" to refer to the system or network of signs and gestures that make social relationships possible, significant, and effective. The social infrastructure is the almost invisible system of connections that gives life functioning power and provides connections and support systems. I take it that the most elemental human infrastructure is a network of stories, sacraments, and signs that give a certain nuance, shape, and possibility to human interaction. An evangelical infrastructure is one that mediates and operates in ways that heal, redeem, and transform. I deliberately use the term "infrastructure" because I refer to something more pervasive and elemental than a belief system or a moral code.[1]

4. While an evangelical infrastructure rooted in the Bible hints at coherence, its construction is not done all at once. I submit that such a construction is a slow, deliberate work done over time, one text at a time. This constructive task is quite like the emergence of a new self through the slow, painful work of psychotherapy. In such sustained work, healing dawns and newness emerges, but only a very little at a time. Thus I suggest the minister must think not of one Sunday or one text as an exercise in "totalism," but each text and each textual offer is a small piece of a larger possibility that will only slowly surface, in ways unhurried.

• II •

In this discussion, I shall take up what I consider to be the large thematics for that infrastructure. As I move along, I will become somewhat more text-specific. In my third chapter, I will move directly to specific texts to indicate some possibilities for this work.

My thesis is a simple one: Negatively, if this evangelical infrastructure is not carefully constructed, the Christian congregation will rely on the dominant infrastructure of consumerism, and will not even discern until very late (too late) that the infrastructure of consumerism contains little good news. Positively, the open situation of the postmodern condition makes such an evangelical construal possible when the church works orally, locally, and in timely ways. I propose simply that ministers proceed with careful intentionality to participate in this wholly new social situation of rival imaginative construals where the church has no formal privilege. I believe that the well-being or deathliness of the human community depends upon the realization or dismissal (or distortion) of this infrastructure.

I will consider three thematics of this evangelical infrastructure that directly counter the dominant infrastructure of military consumerism. The dramatic power of biblical faith is that it is, in large sweep, ordered into a past/present/future, that is, with a life *created* by God and *consummated* by God.[2] This is such a truism in the community of faith that I think we often fail to see how very odd such a claim is, and how crucial it is for the good news of the gospel. It is both odd and crucial when this pattern of affirmation is contrasted with the primary propensity of modern secularism, which believes in neither a creation nor a consummation. The result of the banishment of an ultimate past and future in the modern world, that is, creation and consummation, is that the present is taken with inordinate and uncritical seriousness, if not absolutized.

In what follows I shall urge that the construction of an evangelical infrastructure has as its proximate aim the reframing of human reality away from an absolutizing of the present to an appreciation of the past and future.[3] This turn has the effect of taking the present seriously, but in a very different kind of way. It belongs definitionally to modernity to deny creation and consummation.

Richard Kearney, without any explicit reference to theology, scores the point with great clarity. A historical hermeneutic, he writes,

is one capable of imagining what things might be like *after* postmodernism. And also, of course, what things were like *before* it. As such, the ethical imagination explodes the paralysis of a timeless present, cultivated by our contemporary culture, and informs us that humanity has a duty, if it wishes to survive its threatened ending, to remember the past and to project a future. We cannot even begin to *know* what the postmodern present is unless we are first prepared to *imag-*

ine what it has been and what it *may become*. To abandon this imaginative potential for historical *depth* is to surrender to a new positivism which declares that things are the way they are and cannot be altered; it is tantamount to embracing the postmodern cult of "euphoric surfaces" which dissolves the critical notions of authenticity, alienation, and anxiety in a dazzling rain of "discontinuous, orgasmic instances."[4]

I propose that in a postmodern situation these affirmations of past and future can at least be asserted locally as a proposal for continuing conversation.

• III •

In an evangelical infrastructure, unlike the claims of consumerist perspective, the community operates with a powerful, poignant memory, a memory that affirms that our past has originated through and been kept for us by a faithful, sovereign God who calls into being things that do not exist (Rom. 4:17). The notion of *creation* is endlessly problematic in the world of modernity. It involves us in exasperating questions of creation and science, creation and evolution, the big bang, *creatio ex nihilo*, and so on.[5] All of these latter formulations, however, are attempts to explain what faith takes as an inscrutable mystery of providence. Creation, as understood in the Bible, by contrast, seeks to explain nothing. Creation faith is rather a doxological response to the wonder that I/we/the world exist.[6] It pushes the reason for one's existence out beyond one's self to find that reason in an inexplicable, inscrutable, loving generosity that redefines all our modes of reasonableness.

Moreover, creation faith, as an assertion that all that exists is wrought by the extravagant generosity of God, is reluctant to give reasons for God's intention. It is enough to acknowledge, be awed, and delighted. This incredible past, to which we have only lyrical access, pushes one's *raison d'être* out beyond one's self, thus quickly refusing every notion of self-sufficiency and suiting us for an Other with whom we have by definition to do.[7]

It is useful and conventional enough to consider that there are three zones or dimensions of this providential past that are characterized by God's generosity and the church's amazed gratitude.

1. *The origin of self.* An evangelical infrastructure asserts, affirms, and celebrates that the human self, each precious one, me and all my neighbors, is a product of God's majesty, power, and generosity.[8] That I exist is a reality that is referred outside myself to the mystery of God to which I can only respond in gratitude and doxology. Because I exist, I must sing a song that voices my life in unfettered gratitude. It is of course true that the people of ancient Israel did not know all we know about the scientific elements of reproduction. They did know, however, "where babies come from." And so they told endless stories about the birth of babies.[9] These are regularly stories of visitation that revolve around an announcement of God's resolve for new life. This community celebrates its babies and gives thanks for them. In such a doxological tradition it would not have occurred to anyone to imagine that he was self-made or self-sufficient. Nor could it have occurred to anyone that she be self-securing, either that she must or that she could secure and guarantee her own existence, because all of life is a gift (see Matt. 6:25-33; 1 Cor. 4:7).

The text that we know best concerning the origin of the human person is Gen. 2:7: "God formed the human persons," who are a combination of ordinary "dust of the ground" and the breath that God breathes. Israel knows about babies and about birth. They had watched the moment of spanking in which the newborn inhales breath and in that wondrous moment begins to live and cry and eat . . . and they were amazed. They knew that the baby did not invent that breath. The baby received it, took it in. Such breath is a gift, given from outside the baby and only received by the baby. All our science has not much advanced beyond the wonder that what is needed for life is indeed given.

A more specific statement of this fragile wonder is Ps. 139:13-16:

For it was you who formed my inward parts;[10]
   you knit me together in my mother's womb.
I praise you, for I am fearfully and wonderfully made.
   Wonderful are your works;
   that I know very well.

My frame was not hidden from you,
when I was being made in secret,
intricately woven in the depths of the earth.
Your eyes beheld my unformed substance.
In your book were written
all the days that were formed for me,
when none of them as yet existed.

The psalmist imagines God being present in the very formation of the embryo, as it is formed, knit together, intricately woven, so that only God beheld my "unformed substance." The language is almost eerie in its depth of speaking of the indescribable mystery and hiddenness of new life. God saw me in my preformed state and presided over the initial formation of my life. It is no wonder that the speaker must break out in doxology, for how could God have such patience, attentiveness, wisdom, and gentleness to work this fragileness as "me"? Thus in verse 14, in the midst of this reflection, the speaker turns to doxology. Existence in the presence of God evokes praise!

In Psalm 103, Israel asserts:

For he knows how we were made;
He remembers that we are dust.

The older translation had it, "He remembers our frame." The term "frame" is the same as the word "form" that is used as a verb in Gen. 2:7.[11] God remembers and knows and allows for our risky point of origin. In response, all our life, God treats us with compassion (*rḥm*), like a father has for his children (Ps. 103:13).[12]

Thus the circumstance of our personal point of origin is one of remarkable incommensurability between God's generosity and our fragility. This awareness of fragile origin is crucial to evangelical faith. To recall it is not maudlin or romantic, but it is to assert the enduring and fundamental fragility of human life. In the world of adult knowledge and power, competence, and achievement, we work as hard as we can to deny and overcome our fragility, and thereby to eliminate generosity as a definitional feature and requirement of our life.

The most hard-driving and successful, in terms of money and power, are able best to hide their abiding fragility. Such hiding is an exhausting, self-defeating game, for the more power one has, the more one must acquire to stay on top, and the power we secure is finally never enough. There is little doubt that military might, greedy acquisitiveness, and brutality and abuse are all the outcomes of this terrible self-deception, of needing to pretend against our fragility. The church is the primary place left in our society for the acknowledgment of our previous, undeniable weakness that depends upon uncommon gentleness and generosity. It is that candid reality of weakness and gentleness that will in the end permit the undoing of an abusive, fearful world of the self-sufficient and the formation of a new counterworld of genuine humanness. Note well: The claim for human fragility is not rooted in an awareness of mortality and death.[13] The affirmation of fragility and generosity comes not in the context of death, but in the glorious wonder of birth. There was a time when I was not, and then by the power, goodness, and mercy of God, I was and I am! I did not "evolve," but was loved and named by one even beyond mother and father, a self unashamed, unqualified, naked, beloved, and safe. Let not your heart be troubled!

Peter Doll has noted another crucial function of this creation of the human self.[14] In four proverbs (Prov. 14:31; 17:5; 22:2; 29:13), the wisdom teachers cite the making of the human self by God as the ground for human equity:

> Those who oppress the poor insult *their Maker*,
> but those who are kind to the needy honor him.
> (Prov. 14:31; see 17:5)

> The rich and the poor have this in common:
> The Lord is *the maker* of them all.
> (22:2; see 29:13)

In the presence of this inscrutable mystery, all are equal. One has no cause for leverage over another. Note well it is our notion of self-sufficiency that leads us to imagine our superior worth. When birthed in God's gentle providence, all are equal.

The proclamation of human fragility (notice, not sin) could be the chance for driven persons from a Cartesian world—for example, the world of consumer advertising—to reenter a world of greater humanness and to regroup around what is our important and undeniably true situation. This evangelical claim is an invitation to relinquish in "basic trust," to be able to confess of one's life,

> I do not occupy myself with things
> too great and too marvelous for me.
> But I have calmed and quieted my soul,
> like a weaned child with its mother;
> my soul is like the weaned child that is with me.
> (Ps. 131:1b-2)

In our conventional world, we get caught in a terrible rat race and have no way out. The wonder of a beloved self formed in God's generosity could produce the "dropouts" from the frantic world of self-securing necessary for the coming of God's new regime.

2. *The origin of the world.* Too much has been said and written about the creation of the world, bewitched as we are with scientific categories. Our evangelical infrastructure, I propose, will in the first instant not seek to accommodate scientific learning, but will make its own statement about the character and quality of the world. The news of the gospel concerning the world is that God has ordered the world as a life-giving, joy-producing system of generativity. While human persons have a task of caring for and enhancing the earth, it is not human persons who have made the earth. Creation affirmations regularly end in doxology; when Israel thinks about creation, Israel, and all creatures with Israel, are dazzled, awed, and grateful. I do not denigrate the gains of science in understanding the world. It may be that the wondrous presentations of *National Geographic* and the Nature Channel on TV, which have behind them such careful research, are the best disclosure we have of the mystery and wonder of a fully functioning world that makes life possible. The world is genuinely a home where we are welcomed, cared for, where our needs are supplied in graciousness.

Two texts may be cited, though there are many others that would be appropriate. Psalm 104 is a hymn celebrating creation. The writers of this hymn have paid great attention to the details of creation and are prepared to savor every element of it.[15] That long recital culminates in verse 24:

> O Lord, how manifold are your works!
>   In wisdom you have made them all;
>   the earth is full of your creatures.

In commenting upon the generous system of food production ordained in creation, the psalm asserts:

> These all look to you
>   to give them their food in due season;
> when you give to them, they gather it up;
>   when you open your hand, they are filled with good things.
> (vv. 27-28)

And then, pushing even beyond food production, the psalm comments upon the very breath that lets babies begin, but which also lets trees and grass and streams and wild goats and young lions breathe:

> When you hide your face, they are dismayed;
>   when you take away their breath, they die
>   and return to their dust.
> When you send forth your spirit,
>   they are created;
> and you renew the face of the ground.
> (vv. 29-30)

Everything depends upon the breath of God. When God gives it, the world works. When God withholds it, trees die, rivers dry up, birds vanish. The whole of creation prays, "Take not your holy wind from us," for by it we live (see Ps. 51:11). The picture given is of a pulsing, functioning network, all designed by God as "good" (beautiful), all dependent, all well-supplied. It did not need to be so. Had the wind not been given by God, we would have had only chaos, disordered and incapable of sustaining life. But it is not so. The world works for life.

In the exile Israel imagines the whole of the created world under the aegis of this God who is more powerful than the Babylonian gods:

THE COUNTERWORLD OF EVANGELICAL IMAGINATION •

> It is he who sits above the circle of the earth,
>   and its inhabitants are like grasshoppers;
> who stretches out the heavens like a curtain,
>   and spreads them like a tent to live in;
> who brings princes to naught,
>   and makes the rulers of the earth as nothing.
>   (Isa. 40:22-23)

Notice that in these two verses, a song about the expansiveness of creation takes an odd political turn. The creator of heaven and earth is the lord, guarantor, and creator of earthly princes. All human power in the end is tenuously held only by leave of the creator God.

This poem for exiles makes a remarkable link between the splendor of creation and the prospect for the weak ones of the earth. The two themes are joined in back-to-back verses:

> Have you not known? Have you not heard?
> The LORD is the everlasting God,
>   the Creator of the ends of the earth.
> He does not faint or grow weary;
>   his understanding is unsearchable.
> He gives power to the faint,
>   and strengthens the powerless.
>   (vv. 28-29)[16]

Creation not only works for the powerful, the mighty, and the knowledgeable. It works as well for the faint, the powerless, the hopeless, and the worthless. It works by giving seed to the sower and bread to the eater (Isa. 55:10). It works so that strength is renewed. It is the creation that precludes weariness and faintness, and invites walking, running, and flying.

Evangelical concern may derivatively raise the issue of our terrible disorderedness that issues in unseemly anxiety and in inescapable fatigue.[17] It is a good question to raise in a local parish: Why so driven, so insatiable, so restless? The answer, in this doxological tradition, is that our lives are driven because we are seriously at variance from God's gracious food-giving program. And where there is a variance and a refusal to trust:

youth are faint and weary,
the young are exhausted,
and there is little liberated flying or exhilarated running.
(see Isa. 40:30)

The world does not depend upon us, and the world is not available to us. The world is out beyond us in God's wisdom. It mocks our pitiful efforts at control, mastery, and domination. How odd that to leave off our anxious pursuit of domination, an act that seems like a loss of control, is only to acknowledge that the world is not ours, cannot be ours, and need not be ours. We are able to celebrate it, nonetheless, as God's own beloved world that mediates life to us.

3. *The origin of community.* The third sphere of reframing our memory in relation to creation is that of community. Israel is a gift of God's originary, originating mercy. Israel itself is enough of an incalculable mystery.[18] *Mutatis mutandis,* the formation of Israel invites evangelical reflection upon the church. The church as an alternative community in the world is not a "voluntary association," an accident of human preference. The church as a wedge of newness, as a foretaste of what is coming, as a home for the odd ones, is the work of God's originary mercy. For all its distortedness, the church peculiarly hosts God's power for life.

Several years ago, I was lecturing to a church group in Anderson, South Carolina. It was a small group of ecumenical Christians, cast in a sea of fearful, religious reactionism. My graduate school son was with me, and we reflected upon the church in Anderson. Of course the church there, like everywhere, is fearful, tamed, and compromised. But then we thought, my son and I, imagine Anderson, South Carolina, without the church. Imagine any community without the church. For it is that odd community, knowingly grounded in God's love, that persistently raises human questions of neighbor justice, and that persistently enacts an answer to these questions in love and care.

I am always astonished at what is left on the chalkboard of Sunday school rooms in little churches. Recently I visited my home church in rural Pilot Grove, Missouri, on a quiet Monday afternoon. There on the chalkboard in the church basement, left over from the previous Sunday, was written:

Ecumenism is the move beyond our present identities.

Imagine, in Cooper County, Missouri! The church in a quite specific way is the place where large dreams are entertained, songs are sung, boundaries are crossed, hurt is noticed, and the weak are honored. The church has no monopoly on these matters. Its oddity, however, is that it takes this agenda as its peculiar and primary business. In all sorts of unnoticed places, it is the church that raises the human questions.

Think again how this all came to be. This community of alternative intention did not originate with good human intention, but is birthed of God's own resolve. In the exile, Israel had ample, painful time in which to reflect upon its origin and character. I cite two texts from that exilic reflection, one an assurance, the other a reprimand.

The assurance is in Isaiah 43:

But now thus says the Lord,
he who created you, O Jacob,
he who formed you, O Israel:
Do not fear, for I have redeemed you;
    I have called you by name, you are mine.
When you pass through the waters, I will be with you;
    and through the rivers, they shall not overwhelm you;
when you walk through fire you shall not be burned,
    and the flame shall not consume you....
Because you are precious in my sight,
    and honored, and I love you,
I give people in return for you,
    nations in exchange for your life.

(vv. 1-4)

The poem is addressed to forlorn little Israel in exile, a struggling community of faith without resources. How remarkable that the poem uses cosmic terms of origin to characterize this community: "who created you, ... who formed you."[19] This community is addressed with the quintessential evangelical affirmation: "Do not fear." And then God, the speaker in this poem, proceeds to assert fidelity, solidarity, companionship, love, a resolve to mother all the lost exiles like a shepherd recovering lost sheep (vv. 5-6).

The community in its disarray is about to begin again, as it did the first time.

It began the first time, and each time, because God takes an initiative and gathers folk together for oddness. God gathers together folk like us, rich and poor, liberal and conservative, willing and reluctant, slave and free, and bids all sign on for odd songs and hard commands. In that way a community is formed like none other in the world. There is nothing here of arrogance or virtue or merit, nothing here of despising outsiders or congratulating insiders. There is only an assurance that to be odd in the world is God's intention for this people. And now this weak, exilic community must decide what to do with its oddness.

The reprimand is the less well known text of Ezek. 16:5-15:

No eye pitied you, to do any of these things for you out of compassion for you; but you were thrown out in the open field, for you were abhorred on the day you were born.

I passed by you, and saw you flailing about in your blood. As you lay in your blood, I said to you, "Live! and grow up like a plant of the field." You grew up and became tall and arrived at full womanhood; your breasts were formed, and your hair had grown; yet you were naked and bare.

I passed by you again and looked on you; you were at the age for love. I spread the edge of my cloak over you, and covered your nakedness; I pledged myself to you and entered into a covenant with you, says the Lord GOD, and you became mine. . . . I adorned you with ornaments: I put bracelets on your arms, a chain on your neck, a ring on your nose, earrings in your ears. . . . Your fame spread among the nations on account of your beauty, for it was perfect because of my splendor that I had bestowed on you, says the Lord GOD.

But you trusted in your beauty, and played the whore because of your fame.

This is amazing theater. God passed by this abandoned little baby, thrown out and rejected, still in the untended condition of birth, navel cord not cut, body unwashed and left naked. God willed this nobody to live. When the baby grew to puberty, God, like a protective parent, clothed and dressed her, brought good clothes, paid for a good education, got her well connected—fit to be a queen!

This pitiful baby become queen is Israel. This desperate object of God's love is the community of faith. Israel (and we say the church) had no power for its own life. It is dependent, failed, exposed, vulnerable, without resources. This text of Ezekiel 16 goes on to chronicle the incredible ingratitude and failure of Israel to respond. That failure, however, does not diminish the wonder of the gift.

The first theme of an evangelical infrastructure, I submit, is to reframe life in terms of origins. In modernity, we either do not think about beginning points at all, or we think in terms of achievement that evokes a sense of self-sufficiency and pride or a sense of hopelessness. Very many people in the dominant patterns of reality suffer from profound amnesia. It is the work of the church to counteract amnesia, for when people remember nothing, we can make only the present absolutely true, unaware of a past time unlike the present. And this in turn leads either to self-congratulations over our well-being or to hopelessness over our sorry lot.

This tradition of biblical text has an enormous stake in memory, and the church is the community that gathers to remember. The memory that is useful for the funding of postmodern imagination need not be ordered, coherent, and reasonable. The text is rather like the script of psychotherapy. It brings to consciousness all sorts of odd features from our past that we have repressed. In so doing, it shatters our thin present tense and makes available to us all sorts of materials out of which may be faced and chosen alternative present tenses. The task of ministry is not always to come down heavily on the present. It is enough, sometimes, to be playful in exploring the past. When we do that through this text, we discover that we—self, world, church—are a wondrous creation wrought in mystery and given in great generosity. When our past is hosted in playfulness, our present need not be held so tightly in control. The present is recontextualized for a practice of gratitude. Our past is astonishing, and our present teems with more rich potential than our fearful, arrogant modernity permits us to imagine.

• IV •

In an evangelical infrastructure, unlike the claims of a consumer perspective, the community operates with a powerful vision, a vision that affirms that the future is not yet finished. God has a powerful intention and resolve to bring us to a wholeness not yet in hand. In order that that full newness may be wrought in and for and through us, God must stand over against the present, for this is a God who "brings to nought the things that are" (1 Cor. 1:28), in order that God's intention may be fully realized.

The notion of consummation (*eschaton*) is endlessly problematic in the world of modernity.[20] It invites us to an act of futuring that refuses the closed developmentalism that resists any notion of newness that is deeply discontinuous from the present. Nonetheless, I shall insist that whereas an evangelical infrastructure is deeply committed to "the assurance of things hoped for, the conviction of things not seen," modernity is by definition a practice of hopelessness that may be, depending upon one's circumstance, either a ground for satisfaction and congratulations or a warrant for despair.

Hope, the conviction that God will bring things to full, glorious completion, is not an explanation of anything. Indeed, biblical hope most often has little suggestion about how to get from here to there. It is rather an exultant, celebrative conviction that God will not quit until God has had God's full way in the world. On the one hand, such an affirmation is an antidote to our deep despair that most often can see no way out of our present vexation. On the other hand, such an affirmation of hope is a warning about our self-sufficiency that imagines that in our own power we can have life on our own terms, now or in time to come.

Hope is an act that cedes our existence over to God, in the trusting assurance that God is "able to accomplish abundantly far more than all that we can ask or imagine" (Eph. 3:20). I do not minimize the problematic of this faith affirmation. I invite you to think with me not only about the problematic of speaking of the promise of God in a congregation that expects and wants nothing from God, but also about the nerve required of a minister to speak boldly about such matters, no doubt even in the face of her or his own misgivings rooted in the seduction into modernity.

As with creation, so consummation as a faith affirmation is essentially an act of doxology, which takes its assurance not from anything observable, but from God's own character that issues in God's own promises. Thus I propose that an evangelical infrastructure requires the regular voicing of the most extravagant and outrageous promises of God.

1. *The finished self.* My comments on the finished self are made in the context of two realities. First, at the most practical, intimate level, we all know about the restless dissatisfaction with ourselves that drives us to despair. As with Paul in Romans 7, we intend to do differently and to be differently, but our will is weak and our intention does not endure. We are not on most days whom we want to be. In our society, it is only the busyness and satiation of our values that keep us from dwelling on this reality about ourselves. An evangelical community cannot afford to let the narcotics of dominant society override our deep, anguished sense that we are indeed unfinished selves.[21] Second, there is a great deal of evidence that suggests that the self is indeed a processive phenomenon, that we are underway, and are not a fixed identity.[22] That processive reality, through which we are being relentlessly constituted and reconstituted, provides us access for a way to speak our evangelical affirmation.

In the Old Testament, it is especially the intimate psalms of lament that voice this unfinished self. In these psalms, as Rainer Albertz has shown, the believing self turns to God in profound need and in profound trust, asking God to do for us what we cannot do for ourselves.[23] This very pastoral eschatology is sounded most often in the voice of petition that cedes one's life over to the purpose and power of God.

I shall cite four such prayers:

Psalm 51 is well known to us as a prayer of confession, placed in the mouth of David. In the daring language of creation, this petition says:

> Create in me a clean heart, O God,
>   and put a new and right spirit within me.
> Do not cast me away from your presence,
>   and do not take your holy spirit from me.

> Restore me to the joy of your salvation,
> and sustain in me a willing spirit.
>
> (Ps. 51:10-12)

The speaker asks for a clean heart, a new and right spirit, access to God's own presence, the gift of God's wind, and finally the "joy of your salvation," the sense of well-being and delight that comes with God's faithfulness. This speaker knows what it means to be unformed and deformed by bad choice, impure heart, misguided spirit, misdirected affections. This speaker knows what it means to have one's whole self given away by default, and then to turn to the God who can put life back together again in new creation. There is here no self-help, no New Year's resolution, no easy fix, only candor about being deformed, hope about being reformed, in the language of creation. Note well that the hoped-for newness includes a yearning to be restored to the very presence of God.

Psalm 22, its first part so well known to us, voices the whole drama of a self lost that is voiced to God. It begins with an acknowledgment of utter bereftness:

> My God, my God, why have you forsaken me?
> Why are you so far from helping me, from the words of
> my groaning?
> O my God, I cry by day, but you do not answer;
> and by night, but find no rest.
>
> (vv. 1-2)

There is nothing here of, "How are things going? . . . Fine, pastor." The pivotal reality of life is to be cut off from God's promise, for reasons we do not know. There is no hint that the abandonment is triggered by sin. It may simply be that in freedom God has gone elsewhere. There is some suggestion that God is careless and neglectful. What the speaker knows is that there is no real life away from the presence.

This terrible plea is matched in the resolution of the psalm, the realization of hope that affirms:

> For he did not despise or abhor
> the affliction of the afflicted;

> he did not hide his face from me,
> but heard when I cried to him.
> (v. 24)

The life that could not enter the presence is now given again to see the face. This is the same face of which we regularly speak, that God should cause the light of God's face to shine upon us and give us *shalom.* The petition at the outset of the psalm is an act of hope, knowing that full communion is the measure of being a finished self in the presence of God.

Psalm 73 provides a dramatic recital of a life consumed in alienation, resentment, and envy. The speaker is on his own hook, and his life is diminished:

> But as for me, my feet had almost stumbled;
> my steps had nearly slipped.
> For I was envious of the arrogant;
> I saw the prosperity of the wicked.
> (vv. 2-3)

The turn in the psalm happens only when the speaker goes into the sanctuary of God's presence and has his life reoriented (v. 17). There the speaker "comes to himself" and acknowledges that:

> Nevertheless I am continually with you;
> you hold my right hand.
> You guide me with your counsel,
> and afterward you will receive me with honor.
> (vv. 23-24)

In the end, it is enough that,

> God is the strength of my heart and my portion forever.
> (v. 26)

Psalm 17 contains a long complaint that appeals to God (vv. 1, 2) and that voices rage at enemies (vv. 9-11). In the end the speaker anticipates full fellowship with God:

> As for me, I shall behold your face in righteousness;
> when I awake I shall be satisfied, beholding your likeness.
> (v. 15)

This is a most staggering affirmation, one of the strangest in the Bible. The speaker anticipates seeing God's face, beholding God's very form.

This collection of prayers, to which others could be added, makes clear that the full, hoped-for self is a self who will live in full communion with God, enjoying God's presence, being utterly safe, at home, at peace in God's presence. This affirmation may strike us as odd and offensive, but it belongs to the core of our faith. It is clear, in my judgment, that modernity has almost completely talked us out of this hope. We fear that such an affirmation sounds mystical, or romantic, or otherworldly, or only for those with a particular "spiritual aptitude." That, however, is not the case in the Psalter.

These are the "prayers of the people," ordinary people who recognize their own true character. The true character of human life, so evangelical faith affirms, consists not in buying and selling, not in being right or good. It consists in communion![24] That is what is promised and what is yearned for. These psalms hope for companionship, at-homeness with God. This is not a particularly pious affirmation, but simply a recognition that we are creatures-for-communion. God has created us with a restlessness for that uncommon rest.[25] In an acquisitive society, we have skewed that desire into wantonness and lust of many kinds, but none of these pursuits ever finally satisfies our desire. It is part of the work of the text-driven church to focus once again on what makes the self whole. It is communion that makes whole, and that communion requires disciplines, embraces, and renunciations in order to become available for life with the God who is not cheaply available.

2. *The finished world.* It takes no great notice or imagination to see that the world as a life-giving, food-producing system of interrelations is as yet grossly unfinished. Whether we look at the political-economic-military capacity to brutalize humanity and to terrorize the earth, or whether we look at the dysfunction of the ecosystem, dominated by greed and fear, it is abundantly clear that the world as we know it is not the one called "good," not the one God intended.

It may well be, no doubt is true, that the rehabilitation of the earth requires a transformation of human perspective and policy. In the end, however, evangelical faith confesses that the completion of the earth requires a decisive action of God. This faith affirms not only that such an action is required, but that God in faithfulness will perform it. The most eloquent statement of that requirement and hope is Paul's lyrical affirmation:

> For the creation waits with eager longing for the revealing of the children of God; for the creation was subjected to futility, not of its own will but by the will of the one who subjected it, in hope that the creation itself will be set free from its bondage to decay and will obtain the freedom of the glory of the children of God. We know that the whole creation has been groaning in labor pains until now, and not only the creation, but we ourselves, who have the first fruits of the Spirit, groan inwardly while we wait for adoption, the redemption of our bodies. (Rom. 8:19-23)

The creation is indeed in deep futility. There is within the creation itself, however, an expectation, an insistence, a resolve that this sorry state of futility need not, will not, and cannot persist. That is, the creation has within it hope that leans toward God in desperate, urgent expectation that God will indeed liberate the world from its terrible decay and bondage. Such a lyrical affirmation cannot be easy to utter in a technological society. Pastors, however, do not need to explain. They need only supply the textual material out of which folk will do their own text-authorized imagining. The very creation that decays has ordained within it— because it is God's creation and not "nature"—an urging toward God's newness that is promised and sure.

The Bible thinks very large, well beyond our privatistic, personalistic faith, in its confidence about the renewal and mending of the world. A most comprehensive and majestic scripting of that confidence is in Isa. 65:17-25. This poem is placed in God's own mouth, uttering God's own resolve about the future of the world. God explains nothing, but only asserts. But what an assertion! God will right all wrongs and make a new world possible:

> For I am about to create new heavens
>   and a new earth;
> the former things shall not be remembered
>   or come to mind.

> But be glad and rejoice forever
> in what I am creating;
> for I am about to create Jerusalem as a joy,
> and its people as a delight.
>
> (vv. 17-18)

New heaven, new earth, new Jerusalem, new humanity, wrought only by the power of God.

The poem specifies the newness to come. When God acts for the sake of newness, everything will be changed:

- the cry of grief, mourning, and distress will be ended...no more death (v. 19);

- no more infant mortality (v. 20);

- no more usurpation of property and displacement from home (vv. 21-22);

- no more "absence," but immediate and full communion with God (v. 24);

- no more fracture of creation in hostility (v. 25); and

- no more hurting or destroying (v. 25).

The poem has its eye on the terrible verdicts of Genesis 3, which sound a deep trouble for all the earth, which eventuates in hurt, exploitation, pain, and grief. The troubled condition of the present world is to be overcome (see John 16:33). At last the world will become the world God has always intended—harmonious, productive, at peace. Of course the poem does not tell us how or where or when. It does, however, tell us who. Whereas modernity has eliminated this "Holy Who" from all its calculations, an evangelical alternative begins with and stays focused on the Who who will bring all reality to glad obedience, that is, all things under glorious subjection.

3. *The finished church.* This is a difficult theme, because the church is only an anticipation of the full, promised community of the whole world. It ill becomes the church to announce its own expected completion, because the church itself is not a goal of God's creation. Given that awkward abrasion, however, this tradition of texts does indeed anticipate a people fully turned to God

in glad, joyous communion. Of course this is not talk about any institutional church structure, bureaucracy, hierarchy, or ideology. "Church" here refers to that community, a slice of humanity, that is committed to and participates in God's resolve for a new world.[26]

The Old Testament does not reflect much upon any "perfect," "finished" Israel, but we may cite two texts.[27] In Jer. 31:31-34, the poet anticipates a new community, in time to come utterly reconciled to God. Two matters are important for that community "in the days to come." On the one hand, all members of this community will utterly "know Yahweh"—that is, acknowledge Yahweh as Lord and fully know the Torah.[28] In other words, this community is completely attuned to God's intention, as voiced in Torah. On the other hand, this community is fully and completely forgiven, no longer immobilized by its residue of old disobedience, and so completely free for glad, full, joyous obedience.

In the second text, Neh. 12:27-30, in a much more concrete way this community is purified by priestly activity, so that it may come to God in complete joy, unfettered and unburdened.

In the New Testament, we may identify three images that reflect the church fully open to God's will. First, Eph. 5:27 utilizes the priestly imagery like that of Neh. 12:27-30 in anticipation of a church that is "holy and without blemish."[29] Second, the dazzling anticipation of Rev. 21:1-3 echoes Isa. 65:17-25 and uses the metaphor of bride, adorned for her husband, bedecked in every kind of loveliness. Third, in a very different usage, James 1:26-27 links religion that is "pure and undefiled" to social concern:

> If any think they are religious, and do not bridle their tongues but deceive their hearts, their religion is worthless. Religion that is pure and undefiled before God, the Father, is this: to care for orphans and widows in their distress, and to keep oneself unstained by the world.

In all these different ways, the text affirms and anticipates that God has in mind and in heart a new economy of heaven and earth that is quite unlike the present, that is not mortgaged to the present, that is not derived from the present. In God's good time God will override the present. That is a mouthful! It is a mouthful for liberals who have taken on too much of Feuerbach and who believe that "God has no hands but ours." It is a mouthful for conservatives who trust in the God "who changest not." It is an intellectual scandal for modernity, which believes that there will be no new pieces of reality given, that all that remains is to govern well what is and will be, and that all one is left to do is secure as much of reality for oneself as one can.

Notice, however, where we come out, if we are outside this evangelical affirmation. While the evangelical claims are notoriously imprecise and inexact, they are nonetheless profound acts of hope that trust and affirm that what God intends is indeed possible.[30] I have no doubt that without that claim, one is finally left in despair, because at best, one is fated to more of the same.

A *defeated self,* one that cannot embrace the hope, ends in depression, perhaps in suicide, perhaps in cynicism, perhaps in brutality. I have no doubt that the violence so large among us, the violence of visible lawlessness, of covert brutality and harassment, of foreign policy, are all acts of despair where nothing new is expected.

A *defeated world* without hope of newness, driven by an economy of scarcity, eventuates in greed and monopoly, and sets up unbearable discrepancies between haves and have-nots.

A *defeated church* that does not believe its own life can be transformed by the spirit and the word ends in the grudging contentiousness of competing claims and interests, devoid of energy for mission, too worried about control to exhibit the marks of the crucified.

Into this large season of defeat for self, for world, for church, the ministry of the evangel sounds the sounds of hope, hope not governed by our frightened reason, not fettered by our notion of what is possible, but as bold as these unembarrassed texts that we take as promises from the very lips of God. With self, world, and church promised newness, these texts anticipate Wesley's great lyrical petition:

> Finish then thy new creation,
> Pure and spotless let us be;
> Let us see thy great salvation
> Perfectly restored in thee;
> Changed from glory into glory,
> Till in heaven we take our place,

Till we cast our crowns before Thee,
Lost in wonder, love, and praise.

The task of reframing, which addresses the extremities of our life, works at two awesome tasks. On the one hand, by *supplanting amnesia with memory*, it gives back to the congregation its forfeited past. On the other hand, by *supplanting despair with hope*, it gives back to the congregation its future. The gifts of memory and of hope mediated by these texts are not a great, coherent system. The gifts rather are given one text at a time, texts so odd and so alien to us, evoking a world not domesticated by our modernity. The speaking of these texts is an embarrassment even to us, because we also have had our horizon bounded by "the possible," when our lives in the gospel are framed only by the impossible. Nonetheless we speak them.

· **V** ·

My thought is that a community that regularly yields its past to a memory of generous origins in God's good power, and that regularly yields its future to the buoyant intentionality of God's promises, a community that breaks out of amnesia and despair will unavoidably live differently in the present. That is, we will not get very far in reshaping the present until both past and future are boldly reframed. But with reframing of those limits, a reshaping of the present could happen.

Imagine a self, no longer the self of consumer advertising, no longer a self caught in endless efforts of self-security, but a self rooted in the inscrutable miracle of God's love, a self no longer consigned to the rat race, but one oriented to full communion with God—which is its true destiny and rightful home. Imagine such a self present regularly to the scripting of the sermon, present regularly to the sacraments of generosity. And imagine as a pastor being present to that self as it grows, changes, and matures.

I cite three texts concerned with a reframed, reshaped self:

First, Psalm 119 depicts this self as a child of the Torah, fully open to obedience. We have been much too worried about legalism and have not noticed that in authentic Jewish piety, obedience to the Torah is not a burden but a joy. The Torah is a gracious disclosure of God's intention, which precludes endless anxiety about how to live. This self, rooted in memory and powered by hope, may echo the psalm, "Oh, how I love your Torah!" (v. 97). The speaker resolves:

> I will keep your law continually,
> forever and ever.
> I shall walk at liberty,
> for I have sought your precepts.
>
> (vv. 44-45)

It is this law that creates liberty; the meeting of the church is intended to generate exactly that kind of liberty for the self, what Luther in a very different context called "the liberty of the Christian."[31]

Second, in the best-known psalm, the speaker culminates:

> Surely goodness and mercy shall follow me
> all the days of my life,
> and I shall dwell in the house of the Lord
> my whole life long.
>
> (Ps. 23:6)

It is unfortunate that this psalm has largely been relegated to funerals. In fact, the psalm is the voice of one who has arrived at gratitude and at basic trust. This speaker is gladly prepared to live in the house of "goodness and mercy," and would not want to live anywhere else. The speaker has a long memory of goodness and mercy, and lives by the promise of assured goodness and mercy. In such memory and interpretation, the speaker lets the present and hoped-for future be shaped in this particular way. We could imagine an "antipsalm" in which a speaker had no shepherd, no straight paths, no living water, no rod and staff, no oil, no table . . . and so wanted everything. Such a one could never tolerate such a safe, assured place as goodness and mercy, where all our needs are met and where all our well-being is guaranteed.

The third text I cite, perhaps a baptismal text, is Col. 3:5-17.[32] In this text, the old self is "put to death" or "stripped off." The new self is marked by compassion, kindness, humility, meekness, patience.

Such a self overflows in love and forgiveness, and culminates in thanksgiving. This is a self that is overwhelmed by and luxuriates in the new birth wrought by the gospel. Such a self is utterly at variance with present-tense selves who intend no obedience, who entertain no safe future, and who hold on dearly against every reclothing.

Imagine a world, no longer a closed arena of limited resources and fixed patterns of domination, no longer caught in endless destructive power struggles, but able to recall that lyrical day of creation when the morning stars sang for joy, a world no longer bent on hostility, but under God's presence as a place where creatures "no longer hurt or destroy." This world and all its socioeconomic, political processes are placed between wondrous origin and full restitution. Imagine a world where anxious fear has become unnecessary and brutal selfishness is inappropriate. The text I cite for that awesome world is the old one in Gen. 9:8-17. In that text, the world has just come through the terrible onslaught of the flood, come through because God has rethought and recared for the world, and now brings the world under a new, covenantal sign.

The rainbow marks the world of true evangelical discernment. The rainbow is not something romantic for lovers, or even something political for the building of political coalitions. It is rather a statement of God's powerful resolve—ordained by God, it serves to remind God of God's own resolve and promise:

And what a promise! It is a promise

- that seedtime and harvest, cold and heat, summer and winter will come and be utterly reliable;

- that never again shall the earth be threatened; and

- that God will remember the everlasting covenant . . . between God and all flesh that is on the earth.

The world, so says this wondrous text, is utterly safe. The world need only learn to trust this word and this sign, and be at ease. A world that cannot remember and that cannot hope will be brutal and fearful. But the world is now re-signed, re-signified, re-marked—safe, trustworthy, assured.

Imagine a community of faith, no longer in exile, cast loose without memory, no longer exposed without assurance. In the midst of its exile, this community of faith thought that its life with God had come to a wretched ending, without hope or protection. Right in the middle of that terrible exile of loss and abandonment, however, its present is drastically renovated by the poet:

> For a brief moment I abandoned you,
>   but with great compassion I will gather you.
> In overflowing wrath for a moment
>   I hid my face from you,
> but with everlasting love I will have compassion on you,
>   says the LORD, your Redeemer. . . .
> This is like the days of Noah to me:
>   Just as I swore that the waters of Noah
>   would never again go over the earth,
> so I have sworn that I will not be angry with you
>   and will not rebuke you.
> For the mountains may depart
>   and the hills be removed,
> but my steadfast love shall not depart from you,
>   and my covenant of peace shall not be removed,
>   says the LORD, who has compassion on you.
>   (Isa. 54:7-10)[33]

There was indeed a moment of slippage in which God's love failed Israel. That moment, however, is over, over and done with. The present, still in exile, is completely transformed. This radical transformation of the present is quite like the flood narrative. What happens to the world in the flood now happens to Israel in exile: "This is like the days of Noah."[34] Like the days of Noah, we thought ourselves abandoned. Like the days of Noah, we are given a new promise of presence and fidelity. New in this reclaimed presence are the words "steadfast love," "covenant of peace," "compassion." Israel is now healed, reassured, made safe, on its way rejoicing.

The church is always troubled in its abandonment. There is a word to the church in its present-tense trouble. Again these words, like Psalm 23, have unfortunately been preempted for funerals. But there is a word to the church in all its present-tense fearfulness:

> Do not let your heart be troubled. . . .
> I will not leave you orphaned.
> (John 14:1, 18)

The church in its dangerous obedience is endlessly at risk. It is, however, not alone, not bereft, not abandoned.

The poem of Isaiah 54 and the promise of John 14 are "taken" (on "taking" see above p. 16) as trustworthy assurances. That assurance is not unlike the assurance of a mother to a little child: "Fear not, I am with you." The promise is not necessarily visible and physical. It is given only in a sign, a gesture, a word that when trusted makes "then" into "now" and "there" into "here." When the word is believed and received, it makes the present palpably peopled with fidelity that is in, with, and under all the threat. It is a great deal to ask the church at risk to believe and trust in such a word. But it is no more than we ask of a small child. The child must learn to trust mother, as each of us has learned to trust, if we have arrived at all at viable adulthood. In the end, what the church (or the trusting child) has to count on is a gesture of fidelity that in its attentiveness and durability is astonishingly transformative.

· VI ·

The present tense, with its threat and risk, is either peopled with fidelity or it is not. Modernity, in its dread of superstition, has given us an empty present tense because words are banished and we are finally alone, unaddressed.[35] It becomes our desperate, Promethean task to fill that emptiness. When we fill that emptiness alone, on our own terms, in our desperateness, we tend to fill it in less than satisfying ways. We fill it with objects of our own construction, and we want more and more of them. "The fullness of time," wrought by us in our fearfulness, has become a fullness of greed, practiced as acquisitiveness, which is in fact an act of idolatry. The outcome of greed, acquisitiveness, and idolatry is commoditization, the reduction of everything and everyone (including ourselves) to a commodity, a means, an object of control.[36] While commoditization is peculiarly poignant in our own time, Descartes has already offered a harbinger of such instrumentalism that treats "nature" as a commodity.[37] In the end, such instrumentalism is not about anything beyond itself, serving no large purpose, so that the instrument becomes the end. It follows inevitably that when a society has no end larger than its fascination with its means, the human spirit shrivels, and brutality displaces compassion.

In that diseased present tense, the church utters its word about an alternative. It *speaks of a self* that is open to obedience (Psalm 119), satisfied with goodness and mercy (Ps. 23:6), and reclothed in holiness and righteousness (Col. 3:5-17). It *asserts a world* that stands safely under God's good promise (Gen. 9:8-17). It *imagines a church* fully cared for and not orphaned (Isa. 54:7-10; John 14:1, 18). That is, it offers a present-tense self, world, and church that are held safely in the fidelity of a covenant that is not disrupted by our fearfulness, a covenant that decisively reshapes and redefines.

The present construed as covenantal fidelity is not an easy, romantic word about intimacy and "relationships." It bespeaks rather a readiness to receive life from the other, from God and neighbor, rather than from self. Whereas commoditization presents the self as the sufficient and principal actor, covenant hosts the other as the focus of well-being.[38] That trust in the other opens the way for a very different psychology of self, a very different public possibility, a very different ecclesiology. At the heart of the matter, the contrast of *commodity* and *covenant* hinges upon the reliability of the other. And that reliability is known through a rich memory marked by generous origins, and a vivid hope marked by a full, joyous completion. Commoditization knows no reliable other, having scuttled a generous memory and a buoyant hope, and is left with a thin, administratable present. Thus everything depends upon an enduring, palpable fidelity that lives with us and for us through time.

For the purpose of sketching out the chance of the church to voice an evangelical infrastructure, I have necessarily thematized, and have urged a certain reading of present crisis. I have suggested that our seduction into modernity evokes in us:

- *amnesia* with no memory of our astonishing point of origin,

- *greed, acquisitiveness, and idolatry* that assure a brutalizing present, and

- *despair* with no hope for our destiny or completion.

This "nonsequence" of *amnesia, greed, and despair* is not acted out by most of us blatantly. By discipline, habit, and social pressure, it is kept below the surface of our awareness. There it lives with powerful, distancing cynicism. In the recent past of modernity, amnesia, greed, and despair have exercised a virtual hegemony in our perception of self, world, and even church.

I have proposed that with the collapse of that hegemony and with the chance for other perspectives, the church and its ministers now have an opportunity to voice and imagine a counterworld that lives in and through the text. In facing this task, we should recognize that our voicing, imaging, and sketching are indeed counteracts, a subversion of the dominant perspective so powerful among us. Thus it is counterimagination to:

- *remember* a rich past in the face of entrenched amnesia,

- *entertain a covenantal present* in the face of a regnant commoditization, and

- *hope* a marvelous future in the face of an established, resigned despair.

When the church conducts its liturgy, when the church reads the Bible, when the church declares the gospel, it engages in a counteract, counteracting the world so long dominant among us.

The most important resistance to this evangelical counterimagination does not come from militant secularists. It comes from well-intentioned believers who are infected with modernity. It comes from the pastor's own sinking sense that none of this is true. So we worship and proclaim:

- a memory in a community that aggressively forgets,

- a covenant in a community deeply enmeshed in commodity, and

- a hope in a community that believes very little is promised or possible.

We imagine it all differently. We "take" it all differently. When we "take" it and imagine it differently, we can (and will) act differently, personally and publicly. Our alternative "as" asserts that the world is much more supple than we had been led to discern. We therefore take a position of advocacy for God's assured newness.

In doing this, we reenact in timid, fearful ways the One whose hour had come. The Fourth Evangelist says of him:

> Jesus, knowing that the Father had given all things into his hands, and that he had come from God and was going to God, got up from the table, took off his outer robe, and tied a towel around himself. (John 13:3-4)

He knew from where he had come, and so do we. He knew where he was going, and so do we. He took a towel, and so do we. He and we fill the present with covenantal acts of compassion and reconciliation. All but one in the room that night embraced the counterimagination of Jesus. In a quite practical way, that counter-imagination lives with power only in the mystery of worship and on the daring lips of the preacher. Worship enacts and preaching voices an offer of new life, against the resilient hegemony of death.

Inside the Counterdrama

THUS FAR I have attempted to characterize a postmodern situation in which imagination of an alternative kind could be freshly undertaken. I have sought, in a thematic way, to sketch out a shape for an evangelical infrastructure and to contrast it sharply with the infrastructure of commodity consumerism. I have only hinted at the role of the Bible in funding this work of counterimagination. I have dropped enough hints, however, so that it is likely clear that I believe the Bible is the pivotal element in the scenario I have been sketching. Moreover, the role of the Bible is crucial in this enterprise, in my judgment, because the Bible is "the live Word of God."[1] That is, I am prepared to "take" the Bible, in all its problematic character, "as" the word of God. Of course I am not unaware that this phrasing is enormously difficult. I hope, however, that as my argument proceeds, it will be clear enough what this "taking as" permits, requires, and entails.

· I ·

In my last chapter I attempted to thematize an evangelical grid of memory/covenant/hope. My thematization, however, like every thematization, is inevitably reductionist and necessarily glosses over the oddness and specificity of the text. In this discussion, I want to go underneath that thematization to urge that our proper subject in each case is the specific text, without any necessary relation to other texts or any coherent pattern read out of or into the text.[2] This approach requires relishing and paying attention to each text, and lingering over it for the sake of its own claim, which may be strange, odd, or even offensive. It is evident that this approach is congenial to postmodern perspective, as it focuses on "little" stories to the disadvantage of the "great story."[3] Concerning the focus of the little story, I make four preliminary observations:

1. Focus on the little story requires us to be, to some extent, free of systematic perspective, and especially of systematic theology.[4] We have learned to read the Bible in terms of a system of thought, usually either orthodox confessionalism or liberal developmentalism. Such an approach permitted one text to judge and evaluate another, and often to eliminate the "lesser" text. My insistence is that the little story that "does not fit" needs to be honored and taken seriously, like Paul's "lesser members of the body."[5]

2. An accent on the little story also requires us to violate much we have learned in historical criticism. The methods in which we have been schooled inevitably operate with hidden criteria (modern rationalism) that decide beforehand what would be included in a text. This method has devised respectable strategies for disposing of what is unacceptable to the modern consciousness, so that issues of artistry that constitute new reality have been handled either by dismissive labels of literary genre or by source divisions that divide and conquer ironies and contradictions in the text. The outcome of historical criticism is most often to provide a text that is palatable to modern rationality, but that in the process has been emptied of much that is most interesting, most poignant, and most "disclosing" in the text.[6]

3. The imposition of modern critical or systematic theological categories upon the text has led us to read the text according to Hellenistic modes of rationality that have come to have most credibility in the modern world. Such a synthetic, rational approach, however, has required a violation of what is most characteristically Jewish in the text. For Jewish reading honors texts that are disjointed, "irrational," contradictory, paradoxical, ironic, and scandalous. As Susan Handelman has made clear, such "rational" readings violate the text, but they do more than violate.[7] They dis-

miss the text and deny us serious access to the oddity of the text, which is a vehicle for the oddity of God and for the oddity of life in the world. Very much of the liturgy and preaching of the church is "kept" and domesticated, first of all by imperial powers that could not tolerate scandalous particularity, and then by the force of those whose mission it has been, in the name of scholarship or ideology, to deny the texts their dangerous, revolutionary power.

Thus I propose a fresh honoring of the ambiguity, complexity, and affront of the text without too much worry about making it palatable either to religious orthodoxy or to critical rationality. I propose that the church become, in fidelity to its legitimating text, a place of rhetorical disjunction in which the text and its proposed "as" fail to conform to or reinforce the dominant hegemony.[8] My hunch is that a great deal of such a practice is bearable in our society precisely because the biblical text continues to exercise enormous authority among us. That is, one can risk this in the church precisely because it is the Bible. This approach, however, requires interpreters of the text to unlearn much that we have valued, much that has made us respectable in the church and in the academy. Moreover, such a practice destines the church, insofar as it takes the text seriously, to give up much of its preoccupation with great metaphysical reality and great moral certitude. After all, if God has been mediated to us through Jewish consciousness and Jewish rhetoric, and if this word is the word of this irrepressibly Jewish God, we might expect enormous epistemological displacement in our characteristically gentile hearing of the text.

4. I suggest, again, that an analogy with Freud's program of psychotherapy is especially helpful.[9] I do not for an instant propose to reduce ministry or textual interpretation to psychoanalytic categories, nor the Bible to psychology. Rather, in four important regards, I refer to the mode of discourse that is characteristically operative in effective Freudian therapy.

First, Freud understood that it is *the surfacing of what ill fits* (e.g., through "Freudian slips"), of what has been repressed and driven underground, that permits a healthy reimaging of life. Thus the parts of the Bible that "do not fit" creedal theology or rational criticism may turn out to be most important. The text voices what ill fits and often offers it to us in the form of details, but we do not sufficiently linger over those details. A good exegete, like a good therapist, will linger over precise wording, the odd incongruity, the repeated accent, in order to notice what commonly remains unnoticed.

Second, Freud understood that it is *in the specificity and in the detail of the conversation* that power for life or for death is lodged. It is not found in the large themes that present the public persona; rather, new life is mediated through the recall of painful, unresolved hurts and wishes. So in the Bible, I propose, the liberating, healing work of the text is not in the grand themes that serve our various reductionisms, but in the acts and utterances that are odd, isolated, and embarrassing.[10] The community, like the analysand, lingers over such moments.

Third, the voicing of the material itself does not yield a new picture of reality. It yields only fresh materials out of which larger thematizations may be reconstituted. Those who take the voiced text seriously *linger as new construals emerge.* In psychotherapy, the two partners to the conversation linger over the voiced material, the remembered dream, the recalled formulation, walk around the voiced material and attend to it. Such a process allows the analysand to continue the process of listening. Very often, the new, odd material yields a disclosure that permits reorientation. It is, however, the hard, demanding, continuing work of interpretation, not merely the reception of the material, that yields newness.

Fourth, there is good reason that we repress material about the self. We have had to, in order to form a viable person. Indeed, our ego-structure is possible only because we censor and select. In the same way, in order to arrive at a workable construal of God, self, and world, we have had to censor and select texts. This is evident in the large portions of the text that receive no hearing in the three-year cycle of the lectionary. And when those censored parts surface, they are dangerously subversive. Indeed, that is why they have been dismissed in the first place. Thus the resurfacing of buried texts subverts one's self-concept and one's memory of family and childhood, and one *must reread everything in light of the newly recovered material.* In parallel fashion, in Bible reading new texts require us to reread everything of God, self, and neighbor in light of neglected texts. Note well that texts, like recovered memories, do not need to be contextualized, placed, or interrelated. They need only be voiced. When voiced, they linger a while, with power, in our imagination.

Now it is my urging that modernity, both as critical finesse and as theological orthodoxy, has required and dictated the loss of many texts, or their necessary misreading.[11] It is easy enough to see, as Robert Carroll sees, that the church has engaged in such misreading, with awareness that some texts are unacceptable.[12] For us schooled in criticism, it is not so easy to see, but equally the case, that scholarly criticism has also, in sophisticated ways, disposed of texts it find unpalatable. Athens and Geneva together have conspired to suppress, and Jerusalem has often been a willing accomplice. That suppression has been in order that the rationalistic hegemony of modernity could prevail, or that the domination of church orthodoxy could control. Our social situation is not unlike the moment of psychotherapy.

Rereading happens only when one discovers that too much has been lost, and the parts that have been systematically preserved and incorporated are not adequate materials out of which to live a life of faith. As a result, one must go back into the material in order to find out what else is there. In a like way, modernity has run its course, and we are having now to reenter exactly those texts so long denied as embarrassing. It is now clear that a managed, self-sufficient, scientific, technological, rationalistic ordering of reality cannot sustain humanness.[13] The brooding underneath must be taken seriously. My urging is that with the biblical text, the church and its ministry are peculiarly positioned to take on that revoicing and reprocessing, which at the same time subverts and retrieves.[14]

• II •

At the beginning of our reflection, I suggest three metaphors that I hope will be useful beyond my governing model of the therapeutic:

1. The Bible is the *compost pile* that provides material for new life.[15] I do not use this figure as an irreverent metaphor to suggest that the Bible is "garbage." Rather, I use it to suggest that the Bible itself is not the actual place of new growth. Our present life, when

we undertake new growth, is often inadequate, arid, or even barren. It needs to be enriched, and for that enrichment, we go back to the deposits of old growth that have been discarded, but that continue to ferment and may contain resources for a way to new life. The Bible consists in biodegradable material that will be willingly cast off, but it can be retrieved. As is often the case with such compost, it contains seeds of its own. It sprouts and grows more than and other than we had in mind. I take this metaphor as an alternative to the notion that the Bible is a guide for the gardener. I think not. Its only guidance is that this material is dangerously generative and that the life it can produce is limited by what is in the deposit. More than that, it does not tell us about the specificity of our life.

2. Each of us in the practice of texts has *a zone of imagination* that stands between the input of the text and the outcome of attitude, belief, or behavior. That is, no treatment of a biblical text moves directly from input to outcome. Anyone who imagines a direct move assumes a neat process and a kind of authority that is not in fact available. That zone of imagination is of course in part shaped by the community. But in fact the personal zone of imagination is a protected place of intimacy and interiority that I keep for my very self, and no one else has access to it. I may on occasion share that interiority with my beloved, my pastor, my therapist, but only rarely and hardly ever fully. It is my quintessential locus where I receive, process, and order all kinds of input, input that heals and assaults, that subverts and transforms, and I take into it and handle what I am able as I am able. It is a place that will not be forced, but works at its own pace. It is that operation of receiving, processing, and ordering that transpires when my mind wonders in listening to a text, a reading, in praying, or in any other time. In that wondrous, liberated moment, I take the material and process it in ways that are useful to me, about which only I know.

About this zone of imagination, I make three observations:

a. It is not, in the moment of receiving a text, empty and unoccupied. It is already a busy, occupied, teeming place, so that the new stuff of the text must mingle, interact with, and compete against what is already there. What is already there is complex. I suggest three characteristic dimensions of the material already at hand. First, there are *powerful vested interests* of mine, about some of which I know. There is no disinterested reception of a text. I regularly have keen antennae to notice how a text touches my vested interest. Second, my vested interest is laid over my *deep fears,* which have long, mostly independent careers. Third, underneath my fears, driving my fears and shaping my interests, are *old, deep, unresolved hurts.* I do believe that the hurt lies at the bottom of my imaginative apparatus. It can of course be argued that this proposed content of the zone is all negative, and one must lay alongside it the great power of hope and joy. My judgment, however, is that our unresolved negativities exercise a more powerful and finally decisive influence upon our capacity to receive and imagine than any positive counterpart.[16]

b. As the text is being offered into this zone of imagination, the input of the text in the church is not the only input, or even the most forceful input. We are able to see, in a postmodern context, that the zone of imagination is beset by a cacophony of rival voices, each of which wants to reshape my imagined world. It is evident that the input of family expectations, peer pressure, economic opportunity, and social ideology of many kinds is operative. It is tempting to make our input from the biblical text sound like these other inputs, perhaps to find allies. My insistence is that this text, in its way of "taking," has no obvious or permanent allies. We must speak in our own voice and idiom, and take our chances with the competition.

c. No one, not the preacher or the interpreter, has any access to this zone of imagination or control over the outcome. We might have thought, in a less sophisticated context, that pastoral care could supervise the entire process from input to outcome. This has never, in my judgment, been the case. For that reason, the pastor or interpreter is enormously free of anxiety about and responsibility for the outcome with the listener to the text. The minister is not the one who must worry about the future, health, or obedience of the listening church. It is the pastor's simple task, given this metaphor, to make sure that the text is offered as input in the liveliest way possible. Beyond that, the subjects themselves must answer for the process.[17]

3. The third image I propose is *exile.* Scholars are now largely agreed not only that we had no biblical text before the exile, but that the exile itself was an evocative force in generating the text.[18]

This critical judgment has enormous metaphorical significance. It suggests that this text (not every text, but this text, and especially the Pentateuch) has a peculiar appropriateness to the exile. This text, then, has its odd authority in a major social displacement. It is a text emerging in and addressed to the emergency of exile, when the political and religious supports of Jerusalem had collapsed.

Mutatis mutandis, I propose that the collapse of modernity, with its loss of white, male, Western, colonial hegemony, is a like situation that may be open to this text. For that reason, the interpreters of this text have an opportunity to offer for imaginative processing exactly this text that has been so unacceptable in more established, stable situations. The text of the Pentateuch does not assume any recoverable supports in Jerusalem. Our interpretation, I suggest, should not assume recoverable supports from the old Western hegemony. It is for that reason that chaos (Genesis 1–2), barrenness (Genesis 12–50), bondage (Exodus 1–15), and wilderness (Exodus 16–18; Numbers 10–36) are the several loci of this text in which Israel imagines itself exposed and vulnerable, but with a holy difference.

These three motifs, *compost pile, zone of imagination,* and *exile,* together suggest that text presentation should not be making the text palatable for a vanished situation of modernity. What is now required and permitted is an evocative, originary assertion that seeks to gather, order, and congeal human reality into a quite new configuration. Israel must leave the garden, leave Ur, leave Egypt, leave Sinai, leave Babylon. Israel is always led, always on the way to newness. The Western church now faces a like departure from old "flesh pots." The text suggests that this traveling, departing people does not travel in safety, but always in vulnerability. But it also does not travel alone. The text invites a memory of "traveling with," a hope of "fellowship with," and a present practice of "communion with." This "being with" liberates, subverts, and finally may overcome the terrible power of numbing commoditization.

• III •

What is now required and permitted is a mode of scripture interpretation quite unlike most of what we have practiced heretofore.

In seeking to find a mode of interpretation congenial to our actual life in the world, I propose that we "take" reality as a *drama,* and that we see the text as a script for that drama.

1. There are dimensions of theater that are immediately suggested by the metaphor of drama, dimensions that I intend for this use of the metaphor of drama:

- There are actors other than me/us, and drama means coming to terms with the "other" who is decisive for how my/our life is shaped.[19]

- In any good drama, there are both character constancy and character development.[20] The character in the third act must be credibly continuous with the character in the first act. In the third act, however, there must have been movement, so that the transaction of the third act is not simply reiteration of the first act.

- In good drama, everything important happens on the stage. That is, all offstage realities must be firmly bracketed out, and the characters are not more than is given on the stage.

- There is of course a script that is fixed and settled. Clearly, however, a good company can render that script in a variety of different ways, so that the same script in fact can yield many different plays, depending upon the freedom and imagination of the players.

I find this notion of drama with its playful open-endedness to be an appropriate counterpart to the epistemology of post-modernity, because drama in life and faith, as drama in theater, need not be so imperialistic and dare not be so absolute. Drama need not claim to voice or enact the whole of truth, but can play with, probe, and explore one moment of truth with patience and courage. It intends, moreover, that this fully exposed moment of enactment should be an opening and a sacrament of everything larger, though it does not claim to grasp all that is larger.

2. Biblical faith as drama may be a way of interpretation peculiarly appropriate to our time and place, a way of interpretation that is alert to two classic dangers. On the one hand, in response to the threat of science, theology in the eighteenth century hardened into a statement of propositional absolutes. In order to fend

off the danger of "absolute" science, faith was ordered into a hard and nonnegotiable set of ideas and concepts that provided a settled, unchanging frame of reference. What now is seen to be a science too self-sure evoked in turn a theology too self-sure.[21] This practice evolved in both Catholic and Reformed circles and eventuated, in the United States, in fundamentalism.[22] The upshot for biblical interpretation is that the Bible had to become a servant of the coded system, and any text that did not accommodate either had to be eliminated or reread, so that the God of the Bible may never do or be anything that violates the closed system.

On the other hand, and no doubt in response to that practice of professed absolutes, along with Darwin and the discovery of developmentalism in the nineteenth century, theology discovered that life, all of life, is a historical process that moves from the simple to the complex.[23] This perspective emphasized the dynamic quality of reality that stood over against every absolute, and moved toward a kind of relativism. With the undermining of ideational absolutes, this way of "liberal" interpretation finally did not need to "take" any claim with final seriousness, because everything is a stage on the way to something else.[24] This perspective eventuated in a kind of liberal urbaneness that came to regard the Bible as one instant in a larger cultural development. The claims of the Bible itself did not need to be treated with final seriousness. As concerns the Bible itself, the claims of faith are transposed into moments in the "history of religion." Conversely, the disclosures of God are moments in God's life along the way, as God becomes more sophisticated and complex.

I am aware that this brief sketch is much too simplistic. For our purposes, it is nonetheless adequate, for it enables us to see that the current "Battle of the Bible" between so-called conservatives and so-called liberals has its root in eighteenth-century *propositionalism* and nineteenth-century *developmentalism,* both of which reflect the faith crisis of their times, but both of which are alien to our own interpretive context and to the claims of the Bible itself. Most scripture scholars, schooled as we all have been in developmentalism, regard the first tendency as the real threat and see the relativism of history as the antidote that saves us from absolutism.[25] My judgment is that one threat is as great as the other. That is, the threat of relativism on the left is as great as that of absolutism on the right, and therefore, the tyranny of academic criticism is no real improvement over the hegemony of ecclesial authoritarianism.

Thus I propose, as a way of moving beyond eighteenth-century absolutism and beyond nineteenth-century developmentalism, that biblical faith as drama for our time and place is a way of reading that respects and takes full account of the text.[26] Moreover, I suggest that faith as drama matches the daily, lived reality of our lives. For in fact, we are not settled, one-dimensional agents. We are in fact characters in many dramas, sometimes trying to bring the parts into a coherent whole, sometimes trying to break out of an oppressive coherence, sometimes exploring a new freedom within that constancy, seeking to guard both against frozenness in which the characters congeal, and against a kind of ad hoc mode of life in which the characters lodge their credibility in fits of incongruity.[27] Reinhold Niebuhr has written a book entitled *The Self and the Dramas of History.*[28] I have wondered if we do not now need a study entitled *History and the Dramas of Self,* because our life is essentially a collage of dramas in which we cope with significant others, in which we struggle for constancy and freedom, and in which we find ourselves endlessly scripted but seeking to act gracefully and freely, to work the script in a new way.

I submit that as we struggle with the fresh rending of the script, so God is also scripted by habit and struggles to rerender the script.[29] Notice, both for us and for God in this drama, all the off-stage issues are bracketed out. This way of reading God's life with us and our life with God is no less serious than eighteenth-century absolutism or nineteenth-century developmentalism. This way of reading, however, focuses on these odd textual moments upon which everything else pivots. Those dramatic moments are judged by no criteria outside the drama itself, for the play is the thing.

3. I submit that this way of reading the text (and reading our life) contains enormously helpful access points for pastoral care. The Bible provides a script (not the only script available) for a lived drama that contains all the ingredients for a whole life.

a. To see my life as a drama (or a series of overlapping dramas) is to insist that my life is not a settled certitude, as though I were painted by number. Nor is my life an empty procession of one damn thing after another. My life is rather an ongoing transaction in which issues of constancy and development (freedom), elements of playfulness, credibility, and danger are all underway. While this drama is one of enormous seriousness, I can indeed trust myself to the drama, for I do not need single-handedly to "make it work." In part, I play against, in the presence of, and supported by the other members of the cast.

b. To see my life as a drama entails recognition of this other character. In the biblical script, God is a genuinely other character who takes a decisive role in the drama.[30] In our postmodern situation, God can hardly be a settled judgment, and God is not a historical "fact." But to "take" God as a dramatic other brackets out all those questions and lets the drama proceed, as it in any case will.

c. To see my life as drama with this other permits me to see that I am a genuine and significant other to God.[31] In a genuine drama, unlike too much pretending piety, the impact of otherness cannot always run in one direction. That is, it will not do to have God always the unimpacted other to us, for that will eventually destroy the drama. To sustain the drama, it is equally necessary that God also should have an other who impinges, and we are that other who makes a difference to the God who is a full participant in the drama. The most obvious place for such impingement is in prayer, which in the Bible is real speech.[32] What is at stake in such a dramatic discernment of faith is the recognition that God does not so dominate the drama that we have no role to play in God's life, but that our own role in the drama has cosmic significance. I should insist that this affirmation of ourselves as *other to God* is characteristic of the Bible, but it is a difficult point for much conventional theology. Moreover, such a dramatic reality correlates with what we know of emotional maturation, as in the development of object relations theory.[33]

4. On the basis of those three elements in the history of interpretation and the history of the self, I propose that in biblical interpretation (in which enterprise I include liturgy, preaching, and teaching), the minister enacts the drama and invites members of the listening, participating congregation to come be in the drama as he or she chooses and is able. That is, preaching in this frame of reference is not for instruction (doctrinal or moral) or

even for advocacy, but it is for one more reenactment of the drama of the text.

In this invitation, the listener is invited to take a role, any role or several roles, to play out that role in secret, or to imagine the lines just beyond those voiced in the script. One may pay attention in order to see how the lines might be rendered, or to see where the lines in the script need to be given different nuance than they presently have or have been conventionally given. As the text is enacted before our eyes (and ears) as a drama in which we may be reluctant spectator or secret participant, the zone of imagination for the listener may be impinged upon, enlarged, healed, jarred, subverted, or even transformed. Much depends on having a good script. Much depends upon the listener being present to the drama. Most, however, depends upon the freedom and courage with which the director plays the script. Notice that in utilizing these categories,

- we avoid the conservative, eighteenth-century question about God's reality offstage; and

- we avoid the liberal, nineteenth-century question about whether this could really happen.

The drama requires for a moment the willing suspension of our disbelief. In the moment of that suspension, we may risk playing the role, hearing the script, and seeing the drama of our life in a wholly new way.

• IV •

The preacher of course has available the very large "drama of salvation" that moves from creation through "fall" to redemption and new life. This scheme in fact is the source of the classical three-point sermon. As Lutherans still largely practice, such a sermon in fact always has the same three points: (1) sin, (2) redemption, and (3) new life. (It is clear that this three-point sermon does not even have a place for creation.)[34] Moreover, this large story is surely the one to which Hans Frei refers when he speaks of "biblical narrative."[35] It is clear that a powerful and long-established case can be made for this story as the core drama of the Bible.

There are, however, important problems with "taking" the Bible solely in terms of this large drama:[36]

1. The immediate, practical problem is that the material is all used up so quickly. Which of us, right out of seminary, has not gone through that script and wondered what else we could preach on?

2. More seriously: To take this one-line drama as the core of biblical faith is excessively systematic and is imposed upon the Bible out of a scholastic grid by those who have never read the Bible closely, or who have not the patience or the attentiveness to linger over the troublesome specificity of the biblical text. The Bible offers many small dramas, some of which are not easily subordinated to the large "drama of salvation."

3. As the Bible does not consist in a single, large drama, but in many small, disordered dramas, so our lives are not lived in a single, large, unified drama. In fact, we are party to many little dramas. In my childhood, I remember a Saturday afternoon radio program entitled "Grand Central Station." It began every week with a dramatic voice that reported the trains sweeping in out of the Hudson Valley. The magisterial voice described Grand Central Station as a "gigantic stage on which are played a thousand dramas daily." Just so in our lives. Our lives are like that. We play "a thousand dramas daily."

In both the Bible and in our lives, there is tension between the large drama and the many little ones that are often unrecognized and unacknowledged. In the Bible, the little pieces that constitute the text do more or less flow toward a central narrative, but not easily, obviously, or uniformly. To make the little pieces fit requires our most heavy-handed, systematic propensity. My argument is that the little dramas of the text need to be taken seriously. In a like way, the little dramas of our lives do not all readily fit into the large, visible drama. Sometimes we deny the small dramas or force them to fit, but on occasion they will cry out for attention to an idiosyncratic element of our self and insist on being taken seriously into account. In pursuing this dramatic mode of interpretation, I am proposing that as we attend to the minor, unincorporated dramas of the Bible, we give folk freedom and permit to attend to the minor, unincorporated dramas of our own life, which are not to be run over roughshod, either by imperial orthodoxy, by imperious ego-structure, or by rationalistic criticism.

• V •

I propose then to take up a number of small texts from a variety of genres and comment on them. My purpose is to reflect upon examples of how texts can be taken up with dramatic freedom if we screen out both the dogmatic grip of the eighteenth century and the historical fascination of the nineteenth century. In considering these texts, taken almost at random, I suggest that impingement upon the zone of imagination is not done in large, compelling, reductionist summaries, but is done one item at a time, one memory, one vision, one image, one narrative at a time, which partly flow together, but not completely. The liturgy will reinforce the unity, and therefore the sermon might well champion the little, unincorporated scripts. The outcome will not be doctrinal or moral coherence. It will be, rather, an energizing, liberating process of imagination that permits us to process the feared, cherished parts of our own life, to process them in the context of this Other who with us traverses the stage and the script.

As we take up these "little" texts, it may become clear that my method (if indeed it is that) seeks to avoid the tyranny of criticism as much as the tyranny of authoritarianism. Thus I propose:

- That these texts do not need to be explained or justified. They need only to be told, as resources for the imagination, left there in that secret zone of intimate reflection to do their own hidden work.

- That such telling, without explanation or rationalization, is easier than the more complicated reasonableness in which we are schooled. The analogy again is that the sermon is not for a university lecture hall with all its careful, protective footnotes, but is as unguarded as a therapeutic conversation in which the unutterableness of the text may be uttered.

- That such unguardedness may permit us to handle "objectionable" texts—texts we do not like, texts with which we may disagree—not because they are true, but because they are our texts, and must be voiced. I propose that in their being voiced, we open to review and transformation other

objectionable scripts that exercise enormous hidden, unacknowledged power over our lives.

- That as we undertake this unguarded telling we move closer
to the voice of the rabbis who offered reality only one text at
a time.[37] In coming closer to rabbinic modes of voicing, we
break with modernist pretensions that want large, settled, coherent truth. As we break with such modernist pretensions,
we may also break with the large cover-ups that are constituted by our imperious ego-structure and our massive social
ideologies. It is into the detailed underneathness that rabbinic
courage leads, and in that underneathness, we may find the
otherness of our own life given back to us.

We take up these texts with the single intention of peopling
imagination freshly with rich supplies of "other" material. This
"other" material does not fit with our old settlements, but it may
generate openings where the new truth of the gospel can have its
say. So to the texts:

Exodus 11:1-9

The LORD said to Moses, "I will bring one more plague upon
Pharaoh and upon Egypt; afterwards he will let you go from
here; indeed, when he lets you go, he will drive you away. Tell
the people that every man is to ask his neighbor and every
woman is to ask her neighbor for objects of silver and gold."
The LORD gave the people favor in the sight of the Egyptians.
Moreover, Moses himself was a man of great importance in
the land of Egypt, in the sight of Pharaoh's officials and in
the sight of the people.

Moses said, "Thus says the LORD: About midnight I will go
out through Egypt. Every firstborn in the land of Egypt shall
die, from the firstborn of Pharaoh who sits on his throne to
the firstborn of the female slave who is behind the handmill,
and all the firstborn of the livestock. Then there will be a
loud cry throughout the whole land of Egypt, such as has
never been or will ever be again. But not a dog shall growl at
any of the Israelites—not at people, not at animals—so that
you may know that the LORD makes a distinction between

Egypt and Israel. Then all these officials of yours shall come down to me, and bow low to me, saying, 'Leave us, you and all the people who follow you.' After that I will leave." And in hot anger he left Pharaoh.

The LORD said to Moses, "Pharaoh will not listen to you, in order that my wonders may be multiplied in the land of Egypt."

In this narrative, Moses and Yahweh reach the final, devastating plague of the exodus. After all else fails, Yahweh finally decides that for the sake of Yahweh's own "firstborn" (see 4:22), Yahweh will kill the firstborn of the empire. In the preliminary part of the narrative, Yahweh announces that it is time for Israel to leave the empire (vv. 1-2). In leaving, God says to Moses, tell the departing slaves to "ask" the Egyptians for their silver and gold. This is a warrant that the newly liberated should seize some of the goods of their erstwhile captors. The silver and gold is owed them, and they are authorized by this tough God to take what is owed them.

The core of the narrative centers in a profound contrast. On the one hand, all the firstborn of Egypt shall die (vv. 4-6). The script pounds with a fourfold "firstborn":

> every firstborn;
> firstborn of pharaoh, even the crown prince;
> firstborn of the female slaves;
> firstborn of the livestock.

All the best, children, slaves, and calves: I mean all!

The response to the killing is predictable—a loud cry, a cry of distress and anguish and rage, a cry from the empire, a cry like which has never been heard and will never be heard. Empires are impervious and do not cry. But this one will. This empire, the hated empire, will sound the quintessential cry, even though the Egyptians thought it could not happen here. This is indeed the first one becoming the last, desolate one, a terrible inversion.

The cry is evoked by the inscrutable, hidden work of God: "About midnight I will go out through Egypt"—at midnight, when no one can see, when empires have their guard down, when pharaoh is vulnerable. You will not see me, and they will not see me, but you will know the outcome, a land struck with horror. In the narrative this will be the first time pharaoh cries, but it will be the second cry in the story as a whole. The very first cry had been on the lips of the Israelites in their oppression: "We groaned and cried out . . ." (2:23; 3:7). Now, at midnight, in vulnerability, the cry has moved, as we never thought it would, from the lips of the slaves to the mouth of the master. The cry has been displaced and reassigned, at midnight, in vulnerability.

And the counterside? Israel, midst all this savage confusion, will sleep soundly (v. 7). Not a dog shall growl. Israel will be completely undisturbed, because the midnight intruder is careful and knowing. The hidden one who savages makes important distinctions. By such care, this agent of death and of peaceful sleep inverts social power. The inversion anticipates the verdict of Jesus in Luke 6:21, 25:

> Blessed are you who cry now,
> for you will laugh. . . .
> Woe to you who are laughing now,
> for you will mourn and weep.

It is a turn of power that is unexpected and inexplicable. Israel arose the next morning to laugh and rejoice in its odd gift of freedom, for the threat of pharaoh was undone in the darkness of the night.

This story moves against our presumed world. It overcomes our presumed, taken-for-granted world by proposing a different one. We had thought there would be no destructiveness or violence for us, certainly not from God. In our big houses we imagined we were immune from threat, protected and secure. We thought "they" would stay in their place, that there would be no Passover, no inversion. We thought God would not take sides against us, but would be evenhanded and protect the status quo. Or change the perception. We thought, as we bedded down in our huts, that it would be the same in the morning, with more bricks to make. We never imagined there would be a Passover, and we thought if there were crying, it would be us in our misery, one more time. We never thought we would hear pharaoh admit to grief. We never imagined God would notice us, or take our part.

Both parties are stunned by the transformation. When the sun came up, there was an inexplicable *novum* in Egypt-land, a newness that hurt some terribly, that caused dancing among the slaves. This text is exactly a liturgical memory, not more. It invites celebration, but it never lets us go behind the celebration to see what had happened. The text does not explain, because all is hidden. It does not explain, and neither dare we. It is enough for the slaves to hear and ponder. It is enough for severe pharaoh to hear and tremble. The text invites pondering and trembling. It asserts that things are not too stable and may not last past midnight. We are more vulnerable than we had thought.

The story raises hard questions: What kind of celebration is this? Who should celebrate? Who is the God celebrated, and how does this God enter the story of the gods of Western civilization? This drama may indeed reflect no facticity and yield no certitudes. It is nonetheless played out before our eyes, and we may pick a part in the story, any part we like. We could play state-owned silver, or firstborn cow, or a sleeping dog. We could tremble and cry, or wonder and rejoice. And then we will awaken, and find out it is only a liturgic scenario. We might be haunted by a story we do not relish and a God we do not welcome. The word of the Lord; thanks be to God!

Deuteronomy 15:1-11

Every seventh year you shall grant a remission of debts. And this is the manner of the remission: every creditor shall remit the claim that is held against a neighbor, not exacting it of a neighbor who is a member of the community, because the LORD's remission has been proclaimed. Of a foreigner you may exact it, but you must remit your claim on whatever any member of your community owes you. There will, however, be no one in need among you, because the LORD is sure to bless you in the land that the LORD your God is giving you as a possession to occupy, if only you will obey the LORD your God by diligently observing this entire commandment that I command you today. When the LORD your God has blessed you, as he promised you, you will lend to many nations, but you will not borrow; you will rule over many nations, but they will not rule over you.

If there is among you anyone in need, a member of your community in any of your towns within the land that the LORD your God is giving you, do not be hard-hearted or tight-fisted toward your needy neighbor. You should rather open your hand, willingly lending enough to meet the need, whatever it may be. Be careful that you do not entertain a mean thought, thinking, "The seventh year, the year of remission, is near," and therefore view your needy neighbor with hostility and give nothing; your neighbor might cry to the LORD against you, and you would incur guilt. Give liberally and be ungrudging when you do so, for on this account the LORD your God will bless you in all your work and in all that you undertake. Since there will never cease to be some in need on the earth, I therefore command you, "Open your hand to the poor and needy neighbor in your land."

This law in the mouth of Moses proposes a most radical social practice, the regular, scheduled cancellation of the debts of the poor. In that ancient world, poor people who could not pay their debt became bonded slaves of their creditors. Given only economic realities, the poor with unpaid bills of course became permanent debtors, fated forever to debts they could not pay. Against such fated, fateful economic practice, Moses opposes the whole force of the exodus, whereby bondaged slaves are freed, and the whole authority of Yahweh is to advocate of the well-being of the slaves.

Into the closed system of debts and credits, Moses thrusts the radical phrase, "year of release"—a time of cancellation, a moment of economic emancipation. The basic practice of release is neither argued nor justified by Moses. It is simply asserted in verse 1. The remainder of the text is a commentary on verse 1. We may observe three rhetorical features of the text.

1. Most remarkably, this brief text contains five absolute infinitives. This is a grammatical construction not frequently used in Hebrew, whereby the main verb of a sentence is repeated to function as an adverb of intensity. Thus the Hebrew will say "give give," but in translation, the second use of the verb is transposed into an adverb, "really give," so that the first verb is intensified. The five uses are:

if you really obey ("if only," v. 5),
if you really open your hand ("rather open," v. 8),
really lend ("willingly lend," v. 9),
really give ("give liberally," v. 10), and
really open your hand ("open," v. 11).

The five statements express the enormous intensity of Moses and the urgency Israel felt about this command. The intensity and urgency are rooted in an exodus vision of social reality. I suspect the intensity is also an effort to counteract the weight of the "common sense" of the market that believes the poor must pay their debts or must remain bonded. Moses' daring affirmation sets limits to the claim and reason of the market, overriding economic reality with the more elemental reality of human community, human dignity, and human well-being.

2. The second rhetorical feature I have noted is that in verse 4 it is affirmed, "there will be no one in need among us . . . if," whereas in verse 11, it is asserted, "there will never cease to be some in need on the earth." This seeming contradiction has often been highlighted because verse 11 is quoted by Jesus in Mark 14:7. The quote by Jesus has been regularly taken to give verse 11 priority over verse 4, and to sanction our resignation in the continuing presence of the poor. The text itself permits no such resignation, however, but moves in exactly the opposite direction.[38] Verse 11, on the one hand, indicates that because there is an endless supply of the poor, the practice of release is all the more urgent. Verse 4, on the other hand, indicates that this practice really can be effective in breaking cycles of poverty and indebtedness, because its faithful implementation will eventuate in the abolition of poverty. Thus the practice is endlessly urgent (v. 11), and it will work (v. 4).

3. The third feature I note is the observation of verse 9. Moses imagines that a cunning investor might calculate that the year of debt cancellation is near, and for that reason one must not loan to the poor, because the cancellation means there would be no repayment. Moses warns against a "mean thought," that is, an attitude or policy whereby the well-being of the neighbor is overridden by the power of one's economic advantage. Thus Moses penetrates behind prescribed behavior to motivation and attitude. He insists that dollars should not drive out neighbors.

This is an odd text and, at first glance, not very preachable. One could agree that it could apply only in a simple, face-to-face economy. Or there is the endlessly raised, defensive question, "They did not ever really do it, did they?" suggesting the gross impracticality of the law.

But remember, we have urged that these texts are not to be taken prescriptively, but are an offer into our zone of imagination. They invite us to reflect upon the exercise of social power and social leverage that makes some strong and some weak, some worthy and some undeserving. We do indeed hold each other in hock by money and influence, by attitude and action, by property and by speech. We hold mortgage on each other in the family. We practice such destructive leverage between suburb and inner-city, between capital long held and labor so precarious, between developed economies and the Third World. The cycles of poverty, not only economic but also psychological, hold folk in thrall and generate massive despair.

The despair lasts until the vicious cycles are broken. Moses proposes that the breaking can happen by generous, intentional acts that forgo advantage for the sake of communal equity. The congregation is invited to reflect upon social leverage and mortgage, upon advantage and humiliation, upon attitudes driven by mean calculation, and upon actions that can overcome fatedness. This is the community that, before the hour of worship is out, will pray for forgiveness, "as we forgive our debtors." Forgiveness is first of all an economic matter in the Bible, and it concerns exactly the cancellation of debts.[39]

The teaching of Moses is strong, strong medicine, that is, a remedy for a malady. It touches the values of the market economy and suggests that the well-being of the neighbor matters more than profit.[40] This command does not lead to a safe, ideological dispute about capitalism and socialism, but simply focuses upon the powerful claim of the neighbor. The law of Moses challenges our presumed world because we have presumed that debts are debts and must be paid. Now that entire regularized pattern is challenged. The power of indebtedness is subverted in this law. In the cancellation of debts, both parties are freed for a different kind of neighborly transaction, but neighborly actions are impossible when the leverage of credit and debt prevails. The vision of

Moses has enormous economic and political potential. It also suggests that more intimate patterns of unforgiveness can produce a living death. The active, intentional cancellation of debts can lead folk to a new life in Jubilee.[41] The word of the Lord—Jubilate!

1 Samuel 16:1-13

The LORD said to Samuel, "How long will you grieve over Saul? I have rejected him from being king over Israel. Fill your horn with oil and set out; I will send you to Jesse the Bethlehemite, for I have provided for myself a king among his sons." Samuel said, "How can I go? If Saul hears of it, he will kill me." And the LORD said, "Take a heifer with you, and say, 'I have come to sacrifice to the LORD.' Invite Jesse to the sacrifice, and I will show you what you shall do; and you shall anoint for me the one whom I name to you." Samuel did what the LORD commanded, and came to Bethlehem. The elders of the city came to meet him trembling, and said, "Do you come peaceably?" He said, "Peaceably; I have come to sacrifice to the LORD; sanctify yourselves and come with me to the sacrifice." And he sanctified Jesse and his sons and invited them to the sacrifice.

When they came, he looked on Eliab and thought, "Surely, the LORD's anointed is now before the LORD." But the LORD said to Samuel, "Do not look on his appearance or on the height of his stature, because I have rejected him; for the LORD does not see as mortals see; they look on the outward appearance, but the LORD looks on the heart." Then Jesse called Abinadab, and made him pass before Samuel. He said, "Neither has the LORD chosen this one." Then Jesse made Shammah pass by. And he said, "Neither has the LORD chosen this one." Jesse made seven of his sons pass before Samuel, and Samuel said to Jesse, "The LORD has not chosen any of these." Samuel said to Jesse, "Are all your sons here?" And he said, "There remains yet the youngest, but he is keeping the sheep." And Samuel said to Jesse, "Send and bring him; for we will not sit down until he comes here." He sent and brought him in. Now he was ruddy, and had beautiful eyes, and was handsome. The LORD said, "Rise and anoint him;

for this is the one." Then Samuel took the horn of oil, and anointed him in the presence of his brothers; and the spirit of the LORD came mightily upon David from that day forward. Samuel then set out and went to Ramah.

In a quite different genre, this text is a playful narrative that lacks the urgency of the Mosaic law. It begins with an unembarrassed abruptness: "The Lord said to Samuel." The narrator does not wonder how this happened, and we are not required to wonder. We may, in our first hearing, take the opening line as it stands. In so doing, we have opened our own life to a quite new option. There is another character in the drama, one who speaks and whose utterance is both a rebuke of Samuel and a command to Samuel. This character can rebuke and command. In this opening line a voice takes the initiative for the narrative to follow. The imperative of verse 1 dispatches Samuel to Bethlehem to find a candidate for king. While the statement is terse, the intent is immense. Samuel knows, as Yahweh does not acknowledge, there is no vacancy in the office of kingship. Yahweh is sending Samuel on a dangerous political mission. Samuel is to take the first step toward a political coup, to reject established authority and to offer a new, only now identified candidate for power. An idyllic mode of narrative discourse introduces a dangerous, revolutionary political maneuver.

Samuel is quick to sense the danger: "How can I go? . . . Saul . . . will kill me." Samuel's comment is common sense, a response any of us in our timidity might have uttered. Yahweh's assurance to the frightened Samuel is preemptive. God instructs Samuel to lie. He gives Samuel the lines he is to speak in his cover-up. Samuel does not even have to think what to say: "Take a calf and tell them you have come to conduct a sacrifice." (Do not tell them you have come to start a coup.)

Samuel arrives in the village of Bethlehem, the one Micah will champion against hated Jerusalem (Mic. 5:2-5). Samuel is a known entity, and his face is well known. A village is not accustomed to hosting a government official. The elders of the village are appropriately upset (vv. 4-5); it is not unlike getting an envelope from the IRS. Do you come peaceably? Or do you come as a meddling governmental outsider? Such outsiders only want our sons (the draft) and our property (taxes). Outside officials always come to take, never to give. Samuel is ready. He recites the lines Yahweh has given: "I have come to sacrifice." Yahweh's little lie works well to reassure the villagers and to give Samuel room in which to operate.

Samuel proceeds to identify the candidate who is to displace the entrenched Saul (vv. 6-9). Samuel had been too impressed with the appearance of Saul, and now he is too impressed with the appearance of Eliab, the first son of Jesse. Samuel is seduced by a tall media figure. At the behest of Yahweh, the real operative in this encounter, Samuel goes through the list of Jesse's sons. He exhausts the list, no candidate. He asks disbelievingly: Are there others? Well, yes, there is a little boy, the eighth son.

The whole company waits while the little one, so little as not to be given a name, is brought in (vv. 10-13). Samuel knows he must no longer be impressed by appearances, for appearances mislead. He is now at work on behalf of those who are not "the beautiful people." These are the ordinary peasant folk of the village. Even the narrator is supposed to know that appearances do not count. Nevertheless, when this youngest of Jesse arrives, the narrator cannot restrain himself: "What a boy! Ruddy, beautiful, handsome!" Yahweh, however, never notices this appearance. Yahweh had already said in verse 1, "I have provided myself a king." The verb "provide" is *ra ah*, "see." I have seen beforehand. Now when the boy enters, Yahweh says to Samuel, "That's him! That's the one I 'saw.' Anoint him." Samuel, as dutiful as ever, does the anointing, and the coup is initiated.

Then, with the anointing, two things happen. First, the spirit of Yahweh rushes mightily upon David. The wind of God, empowering the little one, comes from out beyond political processes, from God's great reservoir of creative power. The wind comes that is no respecter of political process or established convention. The narrative asserts that this little one is now made larger than life. Second, now for the first time, the little boy, the coming king, is named. It is David! As in a good nominating speech, the name has been withheld by the narrator until the last possible moment. Now all of God's providential intention has settled on this one little boy. A new king will now proceed to the throne.

The story is idyllic, and the boy is innocent. The narrative lives at a safe distance from us, so we are free to enjoy. If we look at the story in context, however, we should not be bewitched by its appearance of innocence. For this narrative, in a cunning and artistic way, invites us to reflect upon a series of subversive affirmations:

- The narrator nimbly inserts Yahweh into the center of the political process. There can be no insistence here against mixing religion and politics. The story is saturated with political intentionality, all revolutionary, all initiated by Yahweh.

- The subject of the story is in fact a coup. Our presumed world affirms that established power is legitimate, for "there is no authority except from God" (Rom. 13:1). Those of us who are settled (tenured) always give the benefit of the doubt to legitimated authority. Here, however, God is the instigator of the revolutionary alternative. This is the God who brings low and also exalts, as mother Hannah sang (1 Sam. 2:7-8). In the face of this God, no established power is safe, for God is in the business of overthrow.

- The mission of Samuel is carried out under the ruse of a religious mission, the offer of a sacrifice. It is a lie on God's own lips that gives to Samuel a safe conduct. Out the window goes our preferred view that God is truthful and does not lie. Indeed, God lies only on important occasions, in acting against established authority too closely allied with the truth. Where the truth has been preempted, lies will work God's dangerous purpose.

- The wind that rushes, the power of God's spirit, creates newness. Our presumed world had trusted that there is no wind that will challenge our trusted structures, or at least that the wind will move through ordered, legitimated channels. This story, however, anticipates the whole threat of Pentecost, when the wind surges and a genuine *novum* is wrought in the earth (Acts 2:1-11).

The interpreter unleashes this narrative into our imagination, and we discover, through the dramatic power of the narrative, that we no longer live in a safe, settled, coherent world, as we had thought. We are more like the village elders who do not want to be disturbed, even by an agent of Yahweh. The narrative, however, happens in spite of our inclination. The intrusion comes upon the wings of a holy lie, the wind blows, and the little one is destined to power. The very last one is on the way to becoming the first one in Israel. Nothing is quite as we had perceived it. Our perceived world is thoroughly shattered when the holy one rebukes and commands and visits. The village of Bethlehem can never go back to a time before the wind had blown. The word of the Lord—right in downtown Bethlehem.

Jeremiah 4:23-26

> I looked on the earth, and lo, it was waste and void;
>   and to the heavens, and they had no light.
> I looked on the mountains, and lo, they were quaking,
>   and all the hills moved to and fro.
> I looked, and lo, there was no one at all,
>   and all the birds of the air had fled.
> I looked, and lo, the fruitful land was a desert,
>   and all its cities were laid in ruins
>   before the LORD, before his fierce anger.

This poetry of Jeremiah plunges us into a much more frightening world. Now it is late—no idyllic narrative, no bright, young king, no surging of the wind that gives life. We are abruptly at "the other end," the terrible termination of a failed monarchy, a compromised temple, and a jeopardized city. Jeremiah looked deeper and saw farther than most. He matched his uncommon sight with his uncommon tongue. He gives us a poem, a poem at the edge of being a vision. He pounds at his listeners, four times, "I looked," four times, "behold," four times a terrible, dreaded emptiness where there had been life.

What he saw no one else had yet seen. He had seen beforehand. God had willed what he had seen, but no poet had yet uttered it. Until the poet spoke, life went on its routine, business as usual, until this utterance. What an utterance!

> Behold . . . waste and void, *tôhû wavôhû*, a return of chaos,
>   no light, a regress to the dark.
> Behold, quaking mountains and trembling hills, everything
>   unstable, reeling in risk.

Behold, no one, not even a bird.
Behold, a desert, a desolation, a wilderness, where there had
been a garden of delight.

The poet is fixed on his beloved Jerusalem, but he is rereading
early Genesis, about light and order, about firmament and birds,
and about creeping things, a garden of delight. Now the poet re-
views the whole recital one more time. All gone! He even knows
the reason: "The LORD, before his fierce anger."

This poem is almost more than we dare to utter, even so long
after its first utterance. Its scope is too large, and its substance
is too ominous. The poet, one element at a time, plucks up and
tears down the whole of the created order, until he has completely
canceled out the whole wonder of creation.

Jeremiah offers us no scientific description, no list of secondary
causes for the destruction. For that reason, the poem is a suitable
offer for imagination. The poem assaults our usual view of a fixed,
stable, safe world, a world majestic in its coherence, functioning
with such regularity and predictability. And besides, we are afraid
of such poetry because it sounds like nutty apocalyptic.

Except . . . the return to chaos is not so remote from our experience—chaos in Eastern Europe, chaos in our inner cities, chaos
in too many parts of our institutional life. Such chaos requires
more police and more dogs and more gates and more lights and
more surveillance. We prattle about terrorists and crime in the
streets. We imagine in our cynical indifference, cynicism to match
that of the ancient royal court of Jerusalem, that somehow we
can maintain little, protected zones of order and safety. The poet,
however, says otherwise. The root cause of the massive threat is
disobedience, greed, indifference, injustice, lack of compassion,
false security, deceptive assurance. We had presumed the world
to be given, and now it comes to us inordinately fragile. We had
taken the world to be morally neutral, just there and functioning, and now it turns out that the world holds large expectations
and Torah demands that cannot be evaded or mocked. The fixed
points tremble and we with them.

Friends of ours went to England to bird-watch. They went to
the sanctuaries of East Anglia and Kent. There were no birds!
Something about a drought, or was it greenhouse? Was it natu-

ral cause or human violation, or divine power? The explanation is mumbled. The locals did not know and could not say. The powers of chaos seem closer than they used to, than they used to be in Jerusalem. There is less and less that can be taken for granted, less and less guaranteed, less given by God, more conditioned by us, consequently, more at risk.

The terms of the poem itself invite us into the precariousness, push us back to the preordered voices of Genesis. We ponder the fierce God who gives nothing cheaply. We notice ourselves, the violators who are skilled in evil, but have long since forgotten how to do good (v. 22). I would not have thought the universe rested its future on our capacity to do good. God called it "very good," but we nullify the adjective with our uncaring refusal, and we make the adverb seem ludicrous. The word of the Lord—look again, and behold.

Isaiah 55:1-3

Ho, everyone who thirsts, come to the waters;
    and you that have no money, come, buy and eat!
Come, buy wine and milk
    without money and without price.
Why do you spend your money for that which is not bread,
    and your labor for that which does not satisfy?
Listen carefully to me, and eat what is good,
    and delight yourselves in rich food.
Incline your ear, and come to me;
    listen, so that you may live.
I will make with you an everlasting covenant,
    my steadfast, sure love for David.

In contrast to Jer. 4:23-26, this poetic unit comes from the other side of the destruction, that is, after the world has turned to disorder. In that disorder, the pseudo-order of the Babylonian Empire has been imposed upon the exiles. It is a demanding, coercive, exploitative order, closely echoing the abuse of the old Egyptian pharaoh. Jews in that orderly disorder seem, however, to have no alternative. For that reason, many of them subscribed to the imperial order. They gave their lives (and their faith) over to imperial productivity. The power and claim of the empire completely outflanked their Jewish faith and their Jewish freedom. The best prospect was to continue such submissiveness to perpetuity.

Into that despairing context of productivity without joy, of satiation without satisfaction, of submission without affirmation comes this odd poem. It begins as a summons, "Ho, everyone who thirsts, come, buy, eat, come buy wine and milk without price." Some think the poem is an imitation of the call of the street vendor who invites people on the street to come taste good food cheap. In this poem, the street vendor is Yahweh. Yahweh, the God of the exodus, is selling (giving away) food the Babylonians do not give at prices the Babylonians would not offer. It is free food that will delight your life.

A street vendor might become somewhat insistent or argumentative. In the second verse, the vendor taunts the Jews in the streets of Babylon: Why do you work so hard for that which does not satisfy? Why do you expect food from the empire that the empire will never give to you? Why do you work so hard for junk food, when gourmet food is ready at hand from me? The vendor contrasts two kinds of food. The contrast is not unlike a TV commercial, between the "product" and "brand X," which is a failure. In this case, brand X is loyalty to the empire, and the "product" that delights is the covenantal freedom and fidelity of Yahweh. Then, like a street vendor, the poet makes the sell. Like a TV commercial, the poem insists upon a response; it insists you buy the product. When you buy this product, you will be well and happy.

The poem requires only a little handling to be poignant for us. We and the people with whom we minister have largely succumbed to the economic demands of our market-driven society. Either we are in production (for the sake of a better life, better home, better education, better . . .) or we are in consumption (more food, more cars, more trade, more sex, more . . .)—all for more and better things in the rat race necessary to the economy. Neither production nor consumption satisfies. We are not more secure, not more at peace, not more content, because that pattern of life cannot give such outcomes, anymore than Babylon can give what we want and need. So why do you stay in the rat race? Why do you labor for that which does not satisfy?

There is an alternative. It is free bread, free milk, free wine,

covenantal food that will not make you rich by Babylonian standards, but will make you whole by covenantal norms. Decide,
and get out of the rat race! Does this mean "dropping out"? Well,
yes, but the street vendor does not coerce. Nor does he specify
how or in what way, or to what extent. Jews and Christians characteristically are indeed people who have always "dropped out"
of coercion and enslavement and despair, and "dropped in" to
covenantal well-being.

The question is a very difficult one for us, but it is very important: Given imperial definitions of reality, how now can we live in
a human, humane way? The answer lies in disciplined disengage-
ment and a full embrace of a new life. The street vendor knows
that all the way from manna to Eucharist, we have taken food to
be a sign, sacrament, and gesture of an alternative. It is an alternative that touches everything, economics as well as liturgy. The
vendor insists upon a choice that requires resistance to junk food,
and offers a chance that anticipates delight.

Clearly this poem flies in the face of the easier, more obvious
assumption that we have to keep the imperial system working, that
we should be responsible for its effectiveness. And anyway, you
only get what you work for. The poet suggests that this definition
of reality is now open to dangerous review. The way of the Lord—
come on over!

Proverbs 15:17

In a quite different genre, I take up one other text concerning
food:

> Better is a dinner of vegetables where love is
> than a fatted ox and hatred with it.

Here, in contrast to Isa. 55:1-3, the text is much more concrete and
specific. Now food first of all means food. It is not a metaphor for
something else. The proverb is formed, as are many such sayings,
as a "better-saying."[42] That is, "this is better than that." As is usual,
the wisdom teacher does not tell why it is better, nor the criteria
for such a judgment. It is better in the judgment of the teacher.
The teacher would say, given his frame of reference, it is obviously

better. It is, of course, not obviously "better" if one stands outside the teacher's frame of reference. Thus the teacher not only instructs, but advocates a specific frame of moral reference.

The saying, as is usual, contrasts two options. The options come from the world of the family table. *Herbs* are better than *fatted ox.* Vegetables are better than roast beef. This could, on the surface, be a cholesterol verdict. It is more than that, however, because the saying adds an addendum to vegetables and beef. Vegetables where love is, beef with hatred. Now it is clear that we are not simply discussing a menu, but we are discussing the world of economic, social assumptions and practices that inevitably go with food. "Vegetables with love" sounds like a life-style and a standard of living that are plain and simple, where people have time for each other. What I would like, however, is to have beef with love. The teacher, however, will not permit such a combination into his teaching.

The teacher precludes "beef with love." Why is that? Because beef is also a signifier, referring to a fast, affluent way of life. Why should that be? Because it takes more energy, more work, more production, more competence, more time, to generate lots of beef for the table. It takes more work, likely two working parents. So imagine that "beef with strife" refers to a busy family in which everyone is hustling to the limit. They arrive home for dinner too tired to care much, too exhausted to communicate, too preoccupied to invest in each other. Frayed nerves lead to worry, which leads to tension, and finally tears.

Now of course I overread the text. What I suggest, however, is very close to the mood of the proverb and to the crisis of many families. The proverb concerns an eating disorder. We now know that individuals do not have anorexia or bulimia; they are disorders that are systemic in families and in societies. Our bodies do not lie: The disorders are signs of a wrongly defined network of social relationships. Thus "beef with strife" refers to a way of life that is excessively ambitious with great cost to the body, the family, and the body politic. But "better"—the teacher suggests "a more excellent way." Stop the destructive ambition, pull back from the seductions of affluence, and enjoy the neighbor. My interpretation holds together the possibility for domestic tranquility and the practice of public good. The two are deeply connected, as this teacher knows very well. There is no domestic tranquility possible while the public good is only a system of acquisitiveness and mutual destructiveness.

This proverb that looks so innocent is in fact a stunning, poignant assault on a taken-for-granted world. That world is one in which we are endlessly committed to the growth of our wealth and the increase of our standard of living. In that world, if one has resources, one is entitled to acquire and eat anything for which one can pay. The teacher already saw what we are now learning about bodily reality. There are limits to the use of our affluence for personal indulgence. The teacher observes that exploitative over-living is damaging not only to our individual bodies, but enormously costly to our family and communal networks. Our choosing between systems of good is not only a pious option. We make choices in more mundane, daily ways. In so doing, we do indeed choose life or death. There are some things we cannot have without other things coming along. In the world of real productivity and real consumption, one cannot have great roast beef without quarreling. You might like it that way, but you cannot have it. This fact redefines the available "better." The word of the Lord—therefore I tell you, do not be anxious.

• VI •

We have considered six texts almost at random, selecting them in order to reflect upon very different genres, each of which enacts for us a strangely alternative world that challenges our commonly assumed world:

1. *Exodus 11:1-9*—A world of disruptive partisanship, against an assumption of God's indifferent neutrality.

2. *Deuteronomy 15:1-11*—A world where human dignity reshapes economics, against an assumption that credit and debt override human possibility.

3. *1 Samuel 16:1-13*—An intruding wind that causes a political coup, against an assumption of God's benign adherence to the status quo.

4. *Jeremiah 4:23-26*—A vision of a world turned back to chaos, against an assumption that the present ordering is endlessly guaranteed.

5. *Isaiah 55:1-3*—An offer of alternative bread, against an assumption that the empire owns the only bread in town.

6. *Proverbs 15:17*—A choice of food and future, against an assumption that we can eat and live any way we want, with impunity.

I am not interested in constructing a systematic alternative to consumerism. Rather, in a postmodern situation, these texts can have a say on their own terms. I draw five conclusions about a text-centered imagination for a postmodern church:

1. The work of "biblical theology" as practiced in the church is *one text at a time.* The texts, one at a time, offer sufficient material and live poignantly close to our life. The transformation we are able to receive in our life is not grand and sweeping, but slow work, like teasing out transformations in therapy.

2. The interpretation of these texts requires a *minimum of historical-critical work.* I have made a few critical assumptions, but not many. The primary requirement for the preacher is not a deep fund of critical expertise, but an evangelical imagination that lets the text touch the operations of our assumed world.

3. The texts characteristically *subvert our usually assumed world.* I do not think I stack the cards to make this point. The texts subvert because they butt up against our unexamined assumptions that are rooted in alien ideology. They do not subvert in a violent way (except perhaps Jer. 4:23-26), but they undermine in the way true discernment always subverts mistaken assumptions.

4. This way of treating the text, as an "army of metaphors," voices the gospel elusively and porously. That is, it does not come down coercively or prescriptively, but *requires the listener to share in the hard work.* As every therapist knows, finally only the other party in the conversation can decide to what extent new insight is permitted to subvert, and in what way. Thus the text and the preacher provide the materials for subversion, but the permission to subvert belongs to the hearer of the text. That is why, in my

judgment, one can fund subversive imagination, but we do not preempt from others the act of imagination.

5. Situated as we are between an old, unexamined world and a new world voiced in the text, located in the moment of subversion where we are quite unsure, we are betwixt and between. Victor Turner's word for that moment is "liminality," a moment between old configurations of reality and new models of reality.[43] It is a moment of deep ambiguity that must be hosted with respect, awe, and patience, not rushed, not precluded, not preempted. It is that precious moment of liminality that makes serious change possible.

As the preacher/liturgist leads the community beyond the hegemony of the white, male, Western world of colonialism, the preacher/liturgist conducts a season of liminality in which the Spirit may bring newness. Such conduct is of course dangerous, if the others come expecting doctrinal certitude or moral absoluteness. But if evangelical affirmation is what is intended, the risk must be run.

In standing before this people who fear and yearn, the preacher/liturgist may take note of the fact that in our desperate, fearful society, most people have few occasions for such liminality, for hosting ambiguity where God's newness is given. Such liminality is given in the arts, but they are mostly limited to certain elite. Such liminality is given in therapy, but that is expensive. For most folk, the moment of worship, the exhibit of visible signs of invisible reality, is the primal place of such liminality. We come to it with the odd expectation that we will be subverted. After all, the reading of the text and the interpretation of the text are claimed to be linked to "the word of the Lord." How uncommon and presumptuous and awesome, in our ordinary round of life, to dare to voice the word of the Lord. It is no wonder, in our weariness and in our confidence, partly out of habit, partly in hopeful passion, that we respond, "Thanks be to God!"

✦ Abbreviations

BR	*Biblical Research*
BZAW	Beihefte zur *ZAW*
CBQ	*Catholic Biblical Quarterly*
EvT	*Evangelische Theologie*
HBT	*Horizons in Biblical Theology*
JBL	*Journal of Biblical Literature*
Int	*Interpretation*
JAAR	*Journal of the American Academy of Religion*
JSOT	*Journal for the Study of the Old Testament*
OBT	Overtures to Biblical Theology
OTL	Old Testament Library
SBT	Studies in Biblical Theology
ZAW	*Zeitschrift für die alttestamentliche Wissenschaft*
ZTK	*Zeitschrift für Theologie und Kirche*

✦ Notes

Chapter 1:
FUNDING POSTMODERN INTERPRETATION

1. On the epistemology of the Enlightenment and the critique mounted against the epistemological claims of religion, see Paul Hazard, *The European Mind 1680–1715* (New York: World Publishing Co., 1963).

2. The strongest frontal assault on historical criticism is that of Walter Wink, *The Bible and Human Transformation* (Philadelphia: Fortress Press, 1973). See the more measured comments of Brevard S. Childs, *Introduction to the Old Testament as Scripture* (Philadelphia: Fortress Press, 1979), chap. 3.

3. See Henning Graf Reventlow, *The Authority of the Bible and the Rise of the Modern World* (Philadelphia: Fortress Press, 1985). For an account of a reaction against criticism, see Jack B. Rogers and Donald K. McKim, *The Authority and Interpretation of the Bible: An Historical Approach* (San Francisco: Harper and Row, 1979).

4. Hazard, *European Mind,* identifies both the brief period of redefinition and the small number of critics who effected the decisive shift into modernity.

5. Stephen Toulmin, *Cosmopolis: The Hidden Agenda of Modernity* (New York: Free Press, 1990).

6. Ibid., 57, 212.

7. Hazard, *European Mind,* suggests that Descartes began as a friend of religion but ended as a destroyer. Indeed, Descartes's *Discourse on Method* is filled with expressions of religious sensitivity, which presumably are to be taken at face value. Toulmin, in contrast to Hazard, does not see Descartes so positively linked to his religious antecedents.

8. Susan Bordo, *The Flight to Objectivity: Essays on Cartesianism and Culture* (Albany: State Univ. of New York Press, 1987).

9. On the rootage of Cartesian "interiority" in the thought of Augustine, see Charles Taylor, *Sources of the Self: The Making of the Modern Identity* (Cambridge: Harvard Univ. Press, 1989), 127–42.

10. Bordo, *Flight to Objectivity*, 76.

11. Ibid.

12. Ibid., chap. 6, 97–118, and esp. 97.

13. A helpful discussion of the issue of gender-biased scientific discourse and a useful bibliography are provided in Brian Wren, *What Language Shall I Borrow? God-talk in Worship: A Male Response to Feminist Theology* (New York: Crossroad, 1989), chap. 2. More generally on the problem, see Helen E. Longeno, *Science as Social Knowledge: Values and Objectivity in Scientific Inquiry* (Princeton, N.J.: Princeton Univ. Press, 1990).

14. On the enduring problems of receding colonialism, witness the residue of the French in Southeast Asia, the British and Dutch in South Africa, and the French and British in the Mideast. Indeed, one can suggest that U.S. foreign policy in all these places has been a sustained, disastrous attempt to conclude or sustain all these scarred results of colonialism.

15. Taylor, *Sources of the Self*, 143–58, has helpfully explicated the role of Descartes in the emergence of modernity. Descartes writes of harnessing the force and the action of fire, water, air, and so on: "We can in the same way employ them in all those uses to which they are adopted, and thus render ourselves the masters and possessors of nature" (*Discourse on Method* [quoted by Taylor, *Sources of the Self*, 149]). Taylor comments on the program of Descartes: "The Cartesian option is to see rationality, or the power of thought, as a capacity we have to *construct* orders which meet the standards demanded by knowledge or understanding, or certainty. . . . For Descartes, the hegemony means what it naturally tends to mean to us today, that reason controls, in the sense that it instrumentalizes desires" (p. 147). And further: "What has happened is rather that God's existence has become a stage in my progress towards science through the methodical ordering of evident insight. God's existence is a theory in my system of perfect science. The center of gravity has decisively shifted" (p. 157).

16. Both Bordo and Taylor refer to the "inwardness" of this mode of knowing.

17. Toulmin, *Cosmopolis*, 30–35.

18. Jane Flax, in a lecture at Cambridge University, has reviewed the way in which the early Enlightenment regarded "action" as the work of men and "words" as the realm of women, so that "men of letters" were anxious about their identity as men. Thus words were "second-rate" and

NOTES TO PAGES 6–8

not to be taken seriously. It is mind-boggling to reflect on the ways in which Foucault has inverted this equation.

19. Toulmin, *Cosmopolis*, 186–92.

20. Langdon Gilkey, *Society and the Sacred: Toward a Theology of Culture in Decline* (New York: Crossroad, 1981), 3–14. See a more or less parallel account by Diogenes Allen, *Christian Belief in a Postmodern World: The Full Wealth of Conviction* (Louisville, Ky.: Westminster/John Knox Press, 1989), 1–19 and passim.

21. Gilkey, *Society and the Sacred*, 6.

22. Ibid., 8.

23. On that programmatic jeopardy, see Michael Harrington, *The Politics at God's Funeral: The Spiritual Crisis of Western Civilization* (New York: Holt, Rinehart, and Winston, 1983).

24. Thomas Kuhn, *The Structure of Scientific Revolutions* (Chicago: Univ. of Chicago Press, 1962). Sallie McFague, *Metaphorical Theology: Models of God in Religious Language* (Philadelphia: Fortress Press, 1982), chap. 3, has provided a convenient exposition of Kuhn, as his work bears upon theological discourse.

25. Scientific study is not only scientific but also political. And insofar as it is political, it is a rhetorical activity. See Herbert W. Simons, ed., *Rhetoric in the Human Sciences* (London: Sage Publications, 1989), and idem, ed., *The Rhetorical Turn: Invention and Persuasion in the Conduct of Inquiry* (Chicago: Univ. of Chicago Press, 1990). In the latter volume, see especially the essays by John Angus Campbell, Alan G. Gross, and Richard Harvey Brown.

26. Michael Polanyi, *Personal Knowledge: Towards a Post-critical Philosophy* (Chicago: Univ. of Chicago Press, 1974).

27. Richard Rorty, *Philosophy and the Mirror of Nature* (Princeton, N.J.: Princeton Univ. Press, 1979), 335, writes: "The application of such honorifics as 'objective' and 'cognitive' is never anything more than an expression of the presence of, or the hope for, agreement among inquirers."

28. The current concern for "political correctness" is germane to this issue. The phrase and the energy about it are almost exclusively a conservative reactionary device to fend off criticism and change. Those same voices were not worried or self-critical as long as their own political and intellectual agenda prevailed and was perceived as "disinterested" and "objective." Thus the accusation of "political correctness" itself is a powerful rhetorical and political gesture, hidden in the ideology of disinterest. See Sheila Briggs, "Buried with Christ," in Regina Schwartz, ed., *The Book and the Text: The Bible and Literary Theory* (Oxford: Blackwell, 1990), 282–303.

29. Jean-François Lyotard, *The Post-modern Condition: A Report on Knowledge* (Minneapolis: Univ. of Minnesota Press, 1984).

30. The literature on the subject is enormous. For a compact presentation of the issues, see J. Severino Croatto, *Biblical Hermeneutics: Toward a Theory of Reading as the Production of Meaning* (Maryknoll, N.Y.: Orbis Books, 1987).

31. See Robert J. Schreiter, *Constructing Local Theologies* (Maryknoll, N.Y.: Orbis Books, 1985).

32. David Tracy, *Plurality and Ambiguity* (San Francisco: Harper and Row, 1989), has provided most helpful categories for responsible theological pluralism.

33. The reason for David Tracy's intense interest in pluralism may indeed be the attempt of Rome to establish its interpretive monopoly in Roman Catholicism. Against such stifling hegemony, pluralism is an important alternative. The same stifling monopoly is yearned for by Allan Bloom, *The Closing of the American Mind: How Higher Education Has Failed Democracy and Impoverished the Souls of Today's Students* (New York: Simon and Schuster, 1987). That deeply ideological book is not a protest against "closing," but against "opening" in ways that disrupt the monopoly long held and long enjoyed by Bloom's ilk. See the comments of Sheila Briggs, "Buried with Christ," 284–85.

34. Karl Marx has succinctly made the point: "The ruling ideas of each age have ever been the ideas of its ruling class." See David McLellan, *The Thought of Karl Marx: An Introduction* (London: Macmillan Press, 1971), 46.

35. Even Robert Carroll, who delights in the objectivity of modern biblical criticism, can concede that "scholars hold to fixed dogmas," but he finally does not recognize that even his claim to objectivity is such an ideological claim. See Carroll, "Ideology," in R. J. Coggins and J. L. Haulden, eds., *A Dictionary of Biblical Interpretation* (Philadelphia: Trinity Press International, 1990), 309–11.

36. On "perspectivism," see the helpful discussion of Jerome Bruner, *Acts of Meaning* (Cambridge: Harvard Univ. Press, 1990), esp. 25–27, 95–96. On the promise and potential of "relativism," see Jean Granden, "Hermeneutics and Relativism," in Kathleen Wright, ed., *Festivals of Interpretation: Essays on Hans-Georg Gadamer's Work* (Albany: State Univ. of New York Press, 1990), 42–62, esp. 46.

37. On "conversation" as a model for doing theology, see not only Gadamer and David Tracy, but also James Cone. Dieter Misgeld, "Poetry, Dialogue, and Negotiation: Liberal Culture and Conservative Politics in Hans-Georg Gadamer's Thought," in *Festivals of Interpretation,* 161–81, suggests *friendship* as a condition enabling much evocative conversation.

38. Paul Ricoeur, *Essays on Biblical Interpretation* (Philadelphia: Fortress Press, 1980), 119–54, has explored the force of "testimony" in asserting theological truth. Less directly on the matter of testimony and truth, see Richard K. Fenn, *Liturgies and Trials: The Secularization of Religious Language* (New York: Pilgrim Press, 1982).

39. The old ideological claim that retirement is time when "the best is yet to be" no longer coheres with economic realities.

40. It was no doubt at the core of Ronald Reagan's political force that he was able to claim that he could embody and maintain that old world and old system. This claim was of course enhanced by a linkage to right-wing religion that is equally reactionary and wistful.

41. This is an outcome of the way in which G. Ernest Wright, *God Who Acts*, SBT 8 (London: SCM Press, 1952), set the categories for interpretation. See also the fuller exposition of those categories by Wright in *The Old Testament and Theology* (New York: Harper and Row, 1969). See my critical response to the "virility of God," in Walter Brueggemann, "Israel's Social Criticism and Yahweh's Sexuality," *JAAR* 45 (1977): 349.

42. It appears to me that the social context of Calvin's high claim of "sovereignty" is not seriously enough taken into account for a proper understanding of Calvin's futures for our own theological work. On continued work in the categories of Reformed faith, see Allan Boesak, *Black and Reformed* (Maryknoll, N.Y.: Orbis Books, 1984), and the comments of Itumeleng Mosala, *Biblical Hermeneutics and Black Theology in South Africa* (Grand Rapids, Mich.: Eerdmans, 1989), chap. 1.

43. The theme of God's pathos has been taken up most programmatically by Jürgen Moltmann, *The Crucified God: The Cross of Christ as the Foundation and Criticism of Christian Theology* (San Francisco: Harper and Row, 1974). Concerning the pervasiveness of the theme in recent theology, see the reservation of Ronald Goetz, "The Suffering God: The Rise of a New Orthodoxy," *Christian Century* 103 (1986): 385–89.

44. The ways in which Jewish modes of thought and speech operate outside of and over against "Western logic" is nowhere more clear than in the works of Emil L. Fackenheim. See especially *To Mend the World: Foundations of Post-holocaust Jewish Thought* (New York: Schocken Books, 1989).

45. Robert P. Carroll, *Wolf in the Sheep Fold: The Bible as a Problem for Christianity* (London: SPCK, 1991), persistently uses the term "modern" for historical criticism in order to suggest that such a rationality is free of the older, debilitating ideological force of tradition. The fact that "modern" criticism can be accepted in such a way indicates its large triumph in interpretation, a triumph that takes itself as "innocent." For a frontal attack on such claimed "objectivity," see Gary A. Phillips, "Exegesis as Critical Praxis: Reclaiming History and Text from a Postmodern

Perspective," *Semeia* 51 (1990): 7–49, and Fred W. Burnett, "Postmodern Biblical Exegesis: The Eve of Historical Criticism," ibid., 51–80. Walter E. Wyman, Jr., "The Historical Consciousness and the Study of Theology," in Barbara G. Wheeler and Edward Farley, eds., *Shifting Boundaries: Contextual Approaches to the Structure of Theological Education* (Louisville, Ky.: Westminster/John Knox Press, 1991), 109, has a very different view of modernist criticism. At least in Old Testament studies, I do not believe historical criticism as conventionally practiced serves "historical consciousness." Indeed, I believe it is its enemy.

46. Thus totalitarian regimes are characteristically frightened by poets who utter liberated speech and generate new social reality. On the political force of speech, see Rebecca S. Chopp, *Power to Speak: Feminism, Language, God* (New York: Crossroad, 1989). Concerning Foucault's understanding of speech as it bears upon biblical interpretation, see Elizabeth A. Castelli, *Imitating Paul: A Discourse of Power* (Louisville, Ky.: Westminster/John Knox Press, 1991).

47. On the constitutive power of rhetoric, see Walter Brueggemann, *Israel's Praise: Doxology against Idolatry and Ideology* (Philadelphia: Fortress Press, 1988), chap. 1.

48. On the power of imagination in evangelical faith, see Garrett Green, "Myth, History, and Imagination: The Creation Narratives in Bible and Theology," *HBT* 12 (December 1990): 19–38, 61–63. Green is here concerned with the role of imagination in the thought of Karl Barth.

49. Amos Wilder, "Story and Story-World," *Int* 37 (1983): 353–64, has sagacious things to say about story-telling as "home-making."

50. Lucy Bregman, "Religious Imagination: Polytheistic Psychology Confronts Calvin," *Soundings* 63 (1980): 36–60, has trenchant comments suggesting that "right brain/left brain" categories have become an ideology that perpetuates the Cartesian dualism.

51. See the meaningful phrase "switching worlds" in Peter L. Berger and Thomas Luckmann, *The Social Construction of Reality: A Treatise in the Sociology of Knowledge* (Garden City, N.Y.: Doubleday and Co., 1967), 157. The practice of counterimagination aims at nothing less than this.

52. Mary Warnock, *Imagination* (Berkeley: Univ. of California Press, 1976).

53. Horace Bushnell identified imagination as a key component in Christian education. See Sharon Parks, "Imagination and Spirit in Faith Development: A Way Past the Structure-Content Dichotomy," in Craig Dykstra and Sharon Parks, eds., *Faith Development and Fowler* (Birmingham, Ala.: Religious Education Press, 1986), 137–56.

54. Garrett Green, *Imagining God: Theology and the Religious Imagination* (San Francisco: Harper and Row, 1989).

55. Ibid., esp. chap. 6.

56. Ibid., 73, 137–45.

57. A wondrous example of an "as" that changes social relations is in a novel by Andre Brink, *A Chain of Voices* (New York: Penguin Books, 1983). In the story, slaves in South Africa hear the rumor that the British are about to invade and free them. On that basis, Brink tells the story of a plantation of slaves who, in anticipation of freedom, rise up and kill their white masters. Moreover, in the epilogue, Brink has the white court conclude that once such an "as" has swept the consciousness of slaves, there is no turning back, and they must be executed.

58. On the radical counterpower of the Abraham-Sarah text, see Walter Brueggemann, " 'Impossibility' and Epistemology in the Faith Traditions of Abraham and Sarah [Gen. 18:1-15]," *ZAW* 94 (1982): 615–34.

59. Elisabeth Schüssler Fiorenza has provided an acute interpretation of the woman who refuses even the claims of Jesus, disputes with him, and forces him to a new position. See her important book, *In Memory of Her: A Feminist Theological Reconstruction of Christian Origins* (New York: Crossroad, 1984), and idem, "Changing the Paradigms," *Christian Century* (September 5–12, 1990): 796–800.

60. David J. Bryant, *Faith and the Play of Imagination: On the Role of Imagination in Religion* (Macon, Ga.: Mercer Univ. Press, 1989).

61. Gordon Kaufman, *The Theological Imagination* (Philadelphia: Westminster Press, 1981). See my guarded comments on Kaufman in *Israel's Praise*, 23–26.

62. Richard Kearney, *The Wake of Imagination: Toward a Postmodern Culture* (Minneapolis: Univ. of Minnesota Press, 1988). See also now his *Poetics of Imagining: From Husserl to Lyotard* (London: HarperCollins, 1991).

63. Idem, "Ethics and the Postmodern Imagination," *Thought* 622 (March 1987): 39–58.

64. Maria Harris, *Teaching and Religious Imagination* (San Francisco: Harper and Row, 1987).

65. This way of discerning reality finally goes back to the work of Ludwig Wittgenstein. In current theological thought, that discernment has become especially important in the work of Hans Frei and George Lindbeck. See the mediating discussion of William Placher, *Unapologetic Theology: A Christian Voice in a Pluralistic Conversation* (Louisville, Ky.: Westminster/John Knox Press, 1989).

66. The joining together of "alternative" and "imagination" is crucial to my argument. It is a point missed by many "liberal activists" who are right about "alternative" but who are impatient with the slow work of imagination, which makes practical alternatives possible. John Dominic Crossan, *The Dark Interval: Towards a Theology of Story* (Allen, Tex.:

Argus Communications, 1975), chap. 3, offered one of the early, most persuasive accounts of the subversive character of parabolic imagination.

67. On the world hegemony of modernity and its profound costs, see Theodore H. von Laue, *The World Revolution of Westernization: The Twentieth Century in Global Perspective* (New York: Oxford Univ. Press, 1987).

68. The confessional claim that God has willed and effected the demise of that hegemony is of course not at all excluded by the identification of more proximate causes. Already in the Old Testament, in the paradigmatic case for ancient Israel, God's will for the demise of Jerusalem is visible only through the operations of the Babylonian Empire. Biblical faith is not at all uneasy about such parallel and overlapping claims.

69. On the power of such reductionisms and on evangelical antidotes, see Walter Brueggemann, *Finally Comes the Poet: Daring Speech for Proclamation* (Philadelphia: Fortress Press, 1989).

70. On the interface of midrashic methods of interpretation and contemporary practices of deconstruction, see Geoffrey H. Hartman and Sanford Budick, eds., *Midrash and Literature* (New Haven: Yale Univ. Press, 1986). Moreover, Freud's psychological iconoclasm is congenial to a peculiarly Jewish hermeneutic of suspicion. See John Murray Cuddihy, *The Ordeal of Civility: Freud, Marx, Lévi-Strauss and the Jewish Struggle with Modernity* (New York: Basic Books, 1974).

71. I have explored the transformative purpose of pastoral care in "The Transformative Agenda of the Pastoral Office," in *Interpretation and Obedience: From Faithful Reading to Faithful Living* (Minneapolis: Fortress Press, 1991), 161–83.

72. See David Harvey, *The Condition of Post-modernity* (Oxford: Blackwell, 1990).

Chapter 2:
THE COUNTERWORLD OF EVANGELICAL IMAGINATION

1. I want to avoid the word "myth," which might often be used for this point. What I intend is more dynamic and more piecemeal than the term "myth" suggests, for the term "myth" has come to mean a stable *structure* of reality. That to which I refer is much less coherent and "imperial" than the usual meaning of "myth."

2. See Martin Buber, "The Man of Today and the Jewish Bible," in *On the Bible: Eighteen Studies* (New York: Schocken Books, 1968), 7, and his reference to Franz Rosenzweig, *The Star of Redemption* (South Bend, Ind.: Univ. of Notre Dame Press, 1985).

3. On "reframing," as it pertains to the theological enterprise, see Donald Capps, *Reframing: A New Method in Pastoral Care* (Minneapolis: Fortress Press, 1990). But see also the reservations by Salvador Minuchin, "The Seductions of Constructivism," *Networker* (September/October 1991): 47–50.

4. Richard Kearney, "Ethics and the Postmodern Imagination," *Thought* 622 (March 1987): 52–53. On a culture characterized by "discontinuous, orgasmic instances," see David Harvey, *The Condition of Post-modernity* (Oxford: Blackwell, 1990).

5. For a recent, comprehensive discussion, see Jürgen Moltmann, *God in Creation: A New Theology of Creation and the Spirit of God* (San Francisco: Harper and Row, 1985).

6. See Terence E. Fretheim, "Creation's Praise of God in the Psalms," *Ex Auditu* 3 (1987): 16–30. The entire issue pertains to the theme.

7. On the cruciality of "the other" for faith, see Emmanuel Levinas, *Totality and Infinity: An Essay on Exteriority* (Pittsburgh: Duquesne Univ. Press, 1969), 27, 33–39, and passim; and Hans Urs von Balthasar, *Theo-drama: Theological Dramatic Theory*, vol. 1: *Prolegomena* (San Francisco: Ignatius Press, 1988), 626, with reference to Ebner, Buber, Marcel, and Rosenzweig. More broadly, see G. A. Johnson, ed., *Ontology and Alterity in Merleau-Ponty* (Evanston, Ill.: Northwestern Univ. Press, 1990).

8. Reference may usefully be made to the first question and answer of the Heidelberg Catechism:

What is your only comfort, in life and in death?
That I belong—body and soul, in life and in death—not to myself, but to my faithful Savior, Jesus Christ, . . . that he protects me so well that without the will of my Father in heaven not a hair can fall from my head. . . .

On birth as a dimension of creation, see Gustaf Wingren, *Creation and Law* (London: Oliver and Boyd, 1961), 83–95.

9. Notice that when the narratives of Genesis are treated as "family stories," as Westermann and Coats are prepared to do, a lot of the memory concerns the wondrous birth of babies. See R. W. Neff, "The Announcement in the Birth Narrative of Ishmael," *BR* 17 (1972): 51–60.

10. The word "formed" here (*qnh*) is not the same as "formed" (*yṣr*) in Gen. 2:7.

11. On the interrelation of Gen. 2:7 and Ps. 103:14, see Walter Brueggemann, "Remember, You Are Dust," *Journal for Preachers* 14 (Lent, 1991): 3–10.

12. On the double use of *rḥm* in Ps. 103:13, see Phyllis Trible, *God and the Rhetoric of Sexuality*, OBT (Philadelphia: Fortress Press, 1978), 33–

34. Trible shows how the image of "father" is reshaped by this term of mother-love.

13. This theme of human fragility and its cover-up resonates with Ernest Becker, *The Denial of Death* (New York: Free Press, 1973), though the language and images here are much more intimate.

14. Peter Doll, *Menschenschöpfung und Weltschöpfung in der alttestamentlicher Weisheit*, Stuttgart Bibel Studien 117 (Stuttgart: Verlag Katholisches Bibelwerk, 1985).

15. The savoring of creation is powerfully voiced by Father Zossema in Fyodor Dostoyevsky, *The Brothers Karamazov* (New York: Quartet Books, 1990), 319: "Love all of God's creation, both the whole of it and every grain of sand. Love every leaf, every ray of God's light. Love animals, love plants, love each thing. If you love each thing, you will perceive the mystery of God in things. Once you have perceived it, you will begin tirelessly to perceive more and more of it every day. And you will come at last to love the whole world with an entire, universal love. Love the animals: God gave them the rudiments of thought and an untroubled joy. Do not trouble it, do not torment them, do not take their joy from them, do not go against God's purpose."

16. For a like linkage between creation and political transformation, see 1 Sam. 2:1-10 and Psalm 146.

17. See Paul Tournier, *Fatigue in Modern Society* (Richmond: John Knox Press, 1965).

18. Martin Buber has written most eloquently on "the mystery of Israel." See his essay, "The Election of Israel: A Biblical Inquiry (Exodus 3 and 19; Deuteronomy)," in *On the Bible*, 80–92. See also Paul M. van Buren, *A Theology of the Jewish-Christian Reality*, pt. 2: *A Christian Theology of the People Israel* (San Francisco: Harper and Row, 1987), pts. 4 and 5, and passim.

19. Rainer Albertz, *Weltschöpfung und Menschenschöpfung*, Calwer Theologische Monographien 3 (Stuttgart: Calwer Verlag, 1974), has persuasively considered the distinction and relation between the creation of the world and the creation of Israel. See also Rolf Rendtorff, "Die theologische Stellung des Schöpfungsglaubens bei Deuterojesaja," *ZTK* 51 (1954): 3–14, and Carroll Stuhlmueller, *Creative Redemption in Deutero-Isaiah*, Analecta Biblica 43 (Rome: Biblical Institute Press, 1970).

20. This problematic is at the heart of Bultmann's hermeneutical program; Bultmann offered a serious proposal to that problematic, and his proposal has turned out to be disastrous for subsequent theology.

21. See Ray L. Hart, *Unfinished Man and the Imagination: Toward an Ontology and a Rhetoric of Revelation* (Atlanta: Scholars Press, 1985). Hart offered one of the first phenomenologies of imagination that has since come to dominate the hermeneutical, anthropological discussion.

From a quite different perspective, see Robert Kegan, *The Evolving Self* (Cambridge: Harvard Univ. Press, 1982).

22. See Walter Brueggemann, *Israel's Praise: Doxology against Idolatry and Ideology* (Philadelphia: Fortress Press, 1988), 18–22.

23. Rainer Albertz, *Weltschöpfung und Menschenschöpfung*, 26–51, and idem, *Persönliche Frömmigkeit und offizielle Religion*, Calwer Theologische Monographien 9 (Stuttgart: Calwer Verlag, 1978), 23–48.

24. As the first answer of the Westminster Catechism asserts, human destiny is to "glorify and enjoy" God.

25. Hoped-for, peaceable communion is enacted provisionally in sabbath rest. See Marva J. Dawn, *Keeping the Sabbath Wholly: Ceasing, Resting, Embracing, Feasting* (Grand Rapids, Mich.: Eerdmans, 1989), and Walter Brueggemann, *Finally Comes the Poet: Daring Speech for Proclamation* (Philadelphia: Fortress Press, 1989), 90–99.

26. In "Praise and the Psalms: A Politics of Glad Abandonment," *The Hymn: A Journal of Congregational Song* 43, no. 3 (July 1992): 14–19 and no. 4 (October 1992): 14–18, I have described the church as "humanity at praise." That is, when the church is taken doxologically (as distinct from institutionally), it is that element of humanity that understands that its purpose in life is to "glorify and enjoy" God.

27. See especially Deut. 18:13; the NRSV renders *tamîm* "remain completely loyal." On the term in Proverbs, see Walter Brueggemann, "A Neglected Sapiential Word Pair," *ZAW* 89 (1977): 234–58.

28. On "knowing," see Hans Walter Wolff, "'Wissen um Gott' bei Hosea also Urform von Theologie," *EvT* 12 (1952/53): 533–54, and more recently Dwight R. Daniels, *Hosea and Salvation History: The Early Traditions of Israel in the Prophecy of Hosea*, BZAW 191 (Berlin: Walter de Gruyter, 1990), 111–16.

29. On the use of the same term in the gospel tradition, see Matt. 5:48; 19:21; and more generally Robert A. Guelich, *The Sermon on the Mount: A Foundation for Understanding* (Waco, Tex.: Word Books, 1982), 234–37.

30. Karl Barth, *Church Dogmatics* (Edinburgh: T. & T. Clark, 1956), 1/2, 13: 1–44, has decisively made the point that theology must move from what is *real* to what is *possible*. Modernity has reversed the process and moved from its notions of the possible to the real, a move sure to erode the claims of faith. On the theme of "impossibility" in the narrative imagination of Israel, see Walter Brueggemann, "'Impossibility' and Epistemology in the Faith Traditions of Abraham and Sarah [Gen. 18:1-15]," *ZAW* 94 (1982): 615–34.

31. Martin Luther, "The Freedom of a Christian," in *Three Treatises* (Philadelphia: Muhlenberg Press, 1960), 262–316.

32. See Philip Carrington, *The Primitive Christian Catechism: A Study in the Epistles* (Cambridge: Cambridge Univ. Press, 1940).

33. On this text, see Walter Brueggemann, *Hopeful Imagination: Prophetic Voices in Exile* (Philadelphia: Fortress Press, 1986), 109–30, and idem, "A Shattered Transcendence? Exile and Restoration," in Steven Kraftchick et al., eds., *Biblical Theology: Problems and Prospects* (forthcoming from Abingdon Press).

34. See Walter Brueggemann, "This Is Like . . . ," *Pulpit Digest* (May/June 1991): 5–8.

35. It is telling that in Jesus' parable on greed (Luke 12:16-21), the greedy man at his celebration celebrates all alone and can only talk to himself. The parable understands, as modernity learns so late, that greed and a passion for commodity isolate and preclude community.

36. See Franz J. Hinkelammert, *The Ideological Weapons of Death: A Theological Critique of Capitalism* (Maryknoll, N.Y.: Orbis Books, 1986).

37. Charles Taylor, *Sources of the Self: The Making of the Modern Identity* (Cambridge: Harvard Univ. Press, 1989), 149, writes of Descartes: "The new model of rational mastery which Descartes offers presents it as a matter of instrumental control. To be free from the illusion which jingles mind with matter is to have an understanding of the latter which facilitates its control. Similarly, to free oneself from passions and obey reason is to get the passions under instrumental direction. The hegemony of reason is defined no longer as that of a dominant vision but rather in terms of a directing agency subordinating a functional domain."

38. Whereas "commodity" is contained in self, covenant concerns the other. On the theme of "alterity," see Levinas, *Totality and Infinity*; George Steiner, *Real Presences* (Chicago: Univ. of Chicago Press, 1989), 146, 188, and passim; and Kearney, "Ethics."

Chapter 3:
INSIDE THE COUNTERDRAMA

1. David Tracy, *The Analogical Imagination: Christian Theology and the Culture of Pluralism* (New York: Crossroad, 1981), 107–15, has taken a foundationalist view of the authority claims of the Bible. For a very different view of its authority, not troubled by establishing "foundations," see George Steiner, "The Good Books," *New Yorker*, January 11, 1988, 94–98.

2. I state this in a most extreme manner. While I am greatly instructed by Brevard S. Childs and his accent on canon, I am resistant to toning down angular texts for the sake of a "coherent" reading.

3. On the failure of the "great story," see Stephen Toulmin, *Cosmopolis: The Hidden Agenda of Modernity* (New York: Free Press, 1990), 186–201; more drastically, Jean-François Lyotard, *The Post-modern Condition:*

A Report on Knowledge (Minneapolis: Univ. of Minnesota Press, 1984); and more programmatically, Jane Flax, *Thinking Fragments: Psychoanalysis, Feminism, and Postmodernism in the Contemporary West* (Berkeley: Univ. of California Press, 1990).

4. I am in no way pejorative toward systematic theology. I suggest only that in a postmodern situation, a different function is now especially urgent, which requires work in more or less unsystematic, piecemeal modes.

5. I am under no illusion that one can be fully free of a larger interpretive frame of reference, but one can take care that the lesser elements are not completely submerged and subsumed.

6. As George Steiner, "Good Books," has observed, the newer literary criticism can also dismiss what is most poignant in a text, in a way very different from the more established historical criticism. The shift to literary criticism is in itself very little gain, if one does not heed the odd, other voice of the text itself with its savage claims. The danger in historical criticism is to make everything past. The danger in literary criticism is to turn serious magisterial claims into aesthetics.

7. Susan A. Handelman, *The Slayers of Moses: The Emergence of Rabbinic Interpretation in Modern Literary Theory* (Albany: State Univ. of New York Press, 1983).

8. The practice of such rhetorical disjunction is definitional for Freudian therapy. The intent of such disjunction is to move underneath the smoothness of reasonable discourse, which conceals. Disjunctive rhetoric, by contrast, is revelatory.

9. See John Murray Cuddihy, *The Ordeal of Civility: Freud, Marx, Lévi-Strauss, and the Jewish Struggle with Modernity* (New York: Basic Books, 1974). Parallels between exposition and such therapeutic conversation are evident in the work of Harold Bloom. See especially Herbert Schneidau, "Biblical Narrative and Modern Consciousness," in Frank McConnell, ed., *The Bible and the Narrative Tradition* (New York: Oxford Univ. Press, 1986), 132–49. Schneidau concludes his essay with an affirmation of "the uncapturability of Yahweh." Freud's program concerns precisely the "uncapturability" of the self.

10. On "therapy" most largely and formidably understood, see Robert E. Cushman, *Therapeia: Plato's Conception of Philosophy* (Chapel Hill: Univ. of North Carolina Press, 1958).

11. On "misreading" as a necessary and inevitable program, see Harold Bloom, *Ruin the Sacred Truths: Poetry and Belief from the Bible to the Present* (Cambridge: Harvard Univ. Press, 1989).

12. Robert C. Carroll, *Wolf in the Sheep Fold: The Bible as a Problem for Christianity* (London: SPCK, 1991).

13. See Herbert Marcuse, *One-dimensional Man: Studies in the Ideology of Advanced Industrial Society* (Boston: Beacon Press, 1968), and Matthew L. Lamb, "The Challenge of Critical Theory," in Gregory Baum, ed., *Sociology and Human Destiny: Essays on Sociology, Religion, and Society* (New York: Seabury Press, 1980), 183–213.

14. On the dialectic of subversion and retrieval, see Tracy, *Analogical Imagination,* chaps. 4–5; Tracy is greatly dependent upon the work of Paul Ricoeur.

15. The figure comes from Stuart Hampshire, *Innocence and Experience* (Cambridge: Harvard Univ. Press, 1989). I have found the reference from a review by John T. Noonan, Jr., in the *New York Times.*

16. See Willard Gaylin, *The Rage Within: Anger in Modern Life* (New York: Penguin Books, 1989).

17. On the limits of the pastoral task, see Ezek. 3:16-21; 33:7-9; and the comment by Moshe Greenberg, *Ezekiel, 1–20,* Anchor Bible (Garden City, N.Y.: Doubleday and Co., 1983), 22:87–97.

18. For a theological exposition of the exilic period, see Peter R. Ackroyd, *Exile and Restoration: A Study of Hebrew Thought of the Sixth Century B.C.,* OTL (Philadelphia: Westminster Press, 1968), and Ralph W. Klein, *Israel in Exile: A Theological Interpretation,* OBT (Philadelphia: Fortress Press, 1979).

19. As concerns God, Barth has made clear that the God of the Bible is "Wholly Other." In conventional interpretation, the accent has been on "wholly," stressing the contrast and discontinuity. When, however, accent is placed on "other," dramatic interpretation can pay attention to the dialectical, dialogical interaction in which each "other" impinges upon its partner in transformative ways. That is, "otherness" need not mean distance and severity, but can also mean dialectical, transformative engagement with.

20. See Dale Patrick, *The Rendering of God in the Old Testament,* OBT (Philadelphia: Fortress Press, 1981).

21. On the complementarity of method in science and theology, see Sallie McFague, *Metaphorical Theology* (Philadelphia: Fortress Press, 1982).

22. See Jack B. Rogers and Donald K. McKim, *The Authority and Interpretation of the Bible: An Historical Approach* (San Francisco: Harper and Row, 1979).

23. The revolutionary events of 1848 decisively changed Enlightenment consciousness. In our purview, this change may be a move from logical rationalism to empiricism or, *mutatis mutandis,* from theological *absolutism* to theological *developmentalism.*

24. Such developmentalism went far in slotting the texts of the Bible in terms of the "history of religion," or even the history of God, sweep-

ing away any sense of the normative or abiding quality of the text. The easy example of such developmentalism is in Harry Emerson Fosdick, *A Guide to Understanding the Bible: The Development of Ideas within the Old and New Testaments* (New York: Harper and Brothers, 1938). That same developmentalism operated in the psychological work of Erik Erikson, though Erikson never imagined that the "early stage" is "outgrown" or superseded. In a rather different way, the same developmentalism is evident in James W. Fowler, *Stages of Faith: The Psychology of Human Development and the Quest for Meaning* (San Francisco: Harper and Row, 1981). For all the claims that these "stages of faith" are descriptive and not formative, it is almost inescapable that they are taken as prescriptive.

25. While this is true of many scholars, Robert Carroll, *Wolf in the Sheep Fold*, has provided a clear and, in my judgment, quite innocent presentation of that assumption.

26. My exploration of dramatic modes of reading that seek to move past absolutism and developmentalism has important parallels to the categories of George Lindbeck, *The Nature of Doctrine: Religion and Theology in a Postliberal Age* (Philadelphia: Westminster Press, 1984).

27. In his spiritual reflections, Baron von Hugel speaks of "the many selves of the self." See also Roberta C. Bondi, *To Pray and To Love: Conversations on Prayer with the Early Church* (Minneapolis: Fortress Press, 1991), chap. 4.

28. Reinhold Niebuhr, *The Self and the Dramas of History* (New York: Univ. Press of America, 1988).

29. On God's struggle with scripted habits, see Walter Brueggemann, "A Shape for Old Testament Theology I: Structure Legitimation," *CBQ* 47 (1985): 28–46, and idem, "A Shape for Old Testament Theology II: Embrace of Pain," *CBQ* 47 (1985): 395–415; the essays also appear in Walter Brueggemann, *Old Testament Theology: Essays in Structure, Theme, and Text* (Minneapolis: Fortress Press, 1992).

30. Concerning "the dialogical principle," see Hans Urs von Balthasar, *Theo-drama: Theological Dramatic Theory*, vol. 1: *Prolegomena* (San Francisco: Ignatius Press, 1988), 626–43.

31. Balthasar, in *Theo-drama*, is most helpful in considering the otherness of the other and the capacity to be other to God.

32. Harold Fisch, *Poetry with a Purpose: Biblical Poetics and Interpretation* (Bloomington: Indiana Univ. Press, 1988), 108–9, writes of the speech of the Psalms: "The Psalms are not monologues but insistently and at all times dialogue-poems, poems of the self but of the self in the mutuality of relationship with the other. . . . The Psalms are not exercises in existential philosophy; we are not speaking of an encounter for the sake of merely discovering the existence of the other and of the self in relation

to the other. The 'Thou' *answers* the plea of the 'I' and that answer sig-
nals a change in the opening situation. . . . The encounter between the 'I'
and the 'Thou' is the signal for a change not merely in the inner realm
of subconsciousness but in the realm of outer events." What Fisch says of
the Psalms is, *mutatis mutandis,* true in general of discourse in the Bible.
This is what Barth means by "realism" about the text.

33. See Walter Brueggemann, "The Costly Loss of Lament," *JSOT* 36
(1986): 51–71. More generally, see Alice Miller, *Thou Shalt Not Be Aware:
Society's Betrayal of the Child* (New York: New American Library, 1986).
More recent developments in object relations theory indicate a new open-
ness to religious faith, with God as a stable object. See Christopher
Bollas, *Forces of Destiny* (London: Free Association Books, 1991), and
J. W. Jones, *Contemporary Psychoanalysis and Religion: Transference
and Transcendence* (New Haven: Yale Univ. Press, 1991).

34. On the cruciality of creation as a category for biblical faith, see H. H.
Schmid, "Creation, Righteousness, and Salvation: Creation Theology as
the Broad Horizon of Biblical Theology," in Bernhard W. Anderson, ed.,
Creation in the Old Testament (Philadelphia: Fortress Press, 1984), 102–
17; and Rolf P. Knierim, "On the Task of Old Testament Theology," *HBT*
6 (December 1984): 91–128. The problem of recovering the theme of
creation appears to be especially acute for Lutherans, as reflected in the
work of Joseph Sittler and Terence Fretheim.

35. Hans Frei, *The Eclipse of Biblical Narrative* (New Haven: Yale
Univ. Press, 1974). Echoing Frei, Ronald F. Thiemann, *Constructing a
Public Theology: The Church in a Pluralistic Culture* (Louisville, Ky.:
Westminster/John Knox Press, 1991), 51, writes: "Scripture, I will ar-
gue, presents a complicated but finally coherent narrative that invites the
reader to consider the world there depicted as the one true reality."

36. This is a major criticism of the whole program of "salvation history,"
which became the story line for the biblical theology movement. That is,
this mode of interpretation is massively reductionist about the richness
of the text. That model was given its normative treatments by Gerhard
von Rad and G. Ernest Wright, but was popularized in such works as
Bernhard W. Anderson, *The Unfolding Drama of the Bible* (Philadelphia:
Fortress Press, 1988).

37. Such a piecemeal notion of truth is stated in radical form by Nietzsche, who wrote in *On Truth and Lie:* "What then is truth? A mobile
army of metaphors, metonymies, anthropomorphisms, in short, a sum
of human relations, which have enhanced, transformed and embellished
poetically and rhetorically and which after long usage seem to a people
to be fixed, canonical, and obligatory" (see Walter Kaufmann, ed., *The
Portable Nietzsche* [New York: Viking Press, 1954], 46– 47).

38. On Jesus' quotation of verse 11, see Michael H. Crosby, *House of Disciples: Church, Economics, and Justice in Matthew* (Maryknoll, N.Y.: Orbis Books, 1988), 118.

39. See Patrick D. Miller, "Luke 4:16-21," *Int* 29 (1975): 417–21; Crosby, *House of Disciples*, 189–91; and more generally, Carter Heyward et al., *Revolutionary Forgiveness: Feminist Reflections on Nicaragua* (Maryknoll, N.Y.: Orbis Books, 1987); and Casiano Floristan and Christian Duquoc, eds., *Forgiveness*, Concilium 184 (Edinburgh: T. & T. Clark, 1986).

40. On the relation of the market economy and social relations, see M. Douglas Meeks, *God the Economist: The Doctrine of God and the Political Economy* (Minneapolis: Fortress Press, 1989), and programmatically, Karl Polanyi, *The Great Transformation* (Boston: Beacon Press, 1957).

41. On the economic implications of the Jubilee, see Marie Augusta Neale, *A Socio-theology of Letting Go: The Role of a First World Church Facing Third World Peoples* (New York: Paulist Press, 1977); John Howard Yoder, *The Politics of Jesus: Vicit Agnus Noster* (Grand Rapids, Mich.: Eerdmans, 1972), 64–77; Crosby, *House of Disciples*, 229–67; and Meeks, *God the Economist*, 88–89. On extrapolations of practical policy, see Richard Cartwright Austin, "Jubilee Now! The Political Necessity of the Biblical Call for Land Reform," *Sojourners* 20 (June 1991): 26–30.

42. See Gerhard von Rad, *Wisdom in Israel* (Nashville: Abingdon Press, 1972), 29; and Graham S. Ogden, "The 'Better'-Proverb (Ṭôb-Spruch), Rhetorical Criticism, and Qoheleth," *JBL* 96 (1977): 489–505.

43. Victor W. Turner, *The Ritual Process: Structure and Anti-Structure* (Chicago: Aldine, 1969), 94–130.

Index of Authors

Index of Scriptural Texts

Old Testament

New Testament